To Rhea,
May some tho
in this book
help to you
when tried.

BORN TO LIVE, BORN TO DIE?

BORN TO LIVE, BORN TO DIE?
An Open Door To The Heart Of A Grieving Mother

by
Shirley J. Earnhart

Layout and design by
Philip Earnhart

SEACHOR BOOKS

Earnhart, Shirley J.
    Born to live, born to die: an open door to the heart
of a grieving mother / by Shirley J. Earnhart. -- 1st ed.
p. cm.

    1. Earnhart, Gregory Dean, 1963-1982. 2. Earnhart,
Shirley J. 3. Bereavement--Psychological aspects.
4. Children--Death--Psychological aspects. 5. Grief--
Psychological aspects. 6. Mothers--Psychology.
I. Title.

BF575.G7E27 2001   115.9'37'0852
                                  QBI01-700566

Library of Congress Control Number: 2001129157

ISBN 0-9711328-0-1

Printed in Canada

All drawings and sketches, including the cover, are by Greg Earnhart

Seasons in the Sun. This permission is granted for the initial print run of 2,500 hardcover and softcover editions printed in the English language. It is understood that a fee for any additional printings must be negotiated prior to release.

Produced by Richard Mort & Associates, Portland Oregon

DEDICATION

THIS BOOK is dedicated to all those
who understood Greg, appreciated
Greg, prayed for Greg and had a part in
guiding him to the river, where God
then led him to the other side. In memory of Gregory Dean Earnhart, honor is
given to all those whom Greg honored.

TABLE OF CONTENTS

PREFACE

MORE THAN NINETEEN YEARS AGO, in April of 1982, Gregory Dean Earnhart left this life to go home to his Creator. This book was started numerous times only to come to a sudden standstill. Just picking up a pen uncovered feelings not yet ready to be expressed or released; grief overruled.

Memories of Greg's short life have been stored in secluded places, treasured by those who knew him. This book exposes a mother's heart and the hearts of those most dear to Greg, even his own. It will permit a glance inside so as to be able to walk along a path of uncertainty, loss, death, grief and fear, as well as joy, hope, love, understanding, faith and life. Come, walk the path, the path through the valley of the shadow of death.

WITH THANKFULNESS

Deep gratitude is expressed to each member of Greg's loving family; his supportive, extended family; and all the caring, faithful friends who shared their hearts with Greg. They all have a part in this book, in their own way. They will read and they will know, for each walked a portion of the path with Greg.

Thank you.

Shirley J. Earnhart
("Shirl")

CHRONOLOGY

July 29, 1963	Gregory Dean Earnhart born in Zürich, Switzerland
1963–1967	Lived in Zürich, Switzerland
1967–1977	Lived in Bern, Switzerland
April, 1977	Moved to Canby, Oregon, USA
June, 1981	Cancer detected
April 21, 1982	Died at home in Canby, Oregon
April 24, 1982	Memorial Service at Canby High School Burial in Salem, Oregon

I
SETTING

1

BORN TO LIVE, BORN TO DIE?

Sometime in the fall of 1962 in Bern, Switzerland, when the trees had turned brilliant colors of orange, gold and red, Greg's life began. His family rejoiced in the prospects of adding another child to their daughter and son. On December 25th, however, miscarriage threatened and his mother was hospitalized for ten days. Alone with her thoughts and fears, she was the only patient in the twelve-bed ward of a quaint, old hospital. Two tall windows overlooked historical buildings, majestic spires and red tile roofs, all glistening with winter snows. The icy river below reflected street lanterns and holiday decorations, while clock and belfry towers rang out the old year and welcomed in the new. Greg's mother waited. Several times a day the doctor's footsteps echoed as he walked through the near empty room to her bed. He told her to rest and wait, assuring her that if the baby was meant to live, it would; time would tell. Only the Creator knew the answer.

On July 29, 1963, Gregory Dean Earnhart was born a healthy, blond, blue-eyed boy. Greg was meant to be born; he was meant

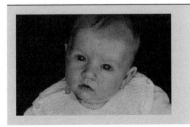

Greg
2 months old
Zürich, Switzerland

to live. There was a plan in this life for him.

As Greg grew, it was evident he was more sensitive than the other children. Scarlet fever hit him hard when he was barely two. Later a near sunstroke threatened his young life. The Swiss called him "zart", which means, delicate. Something else became very evident in the early years of Greg's development. He had a deep love for help-ing others and a creative interest in music and art. He entertained house guests whether they wanted to be or not. Snacks, homemade gifts and a touch of music were all important parts of his presentation.

In school, Greg was a top student in spite of his doodling, whis-pering and wiggling. His teachers labeled him "creative." His mother used the term "one of a kind." She had decided that one Greg was a true blessing, but two with all that energy would have worn her out. Greg was seldom still.

When Greg was about ten years old, his dad built the children a puppet theater. By this time, Greg's older brother, sister and his younger brother were ready to be a part of Greg's first stage crew. The apartment house basement was transformed into a performing arts center, and Greg's original theater group was established. Because of his strong desire to create happiness in others, the Earnhart troupe presented regular shows.

10 years old
Bern,
Switzerland

Greg's enthusiasm was like a flame in the wind, always alive. His happiness was like a childhood disease—everyone caught it. His love for life and for others was like a majestic waterfall, powerful and fulfilling. Yes, God had meant for him to live. There was a purpose.

As Greg turned fourteen, his family faced a very difficult deci-sion. It seemed necessary to leave Greg's place of birth and return to the land of his citizenship, America. Parting was difficult. The fam-ily settled in Oregon, a state with magnificent mountains, towering trees, lush valleys, rushing rivers, vast deserts, and a mighty ocean.

Greg entered junior high, his sister continued in college, his older brother was accepted into art school, one younger brother entered sixth grade, the littlest brother went to kindergarten. Greg became homesick for Switzerland, his friends, and the languages he knew so well. When he was teased because of the way he dressed and talked, his older brother helped him understand that conforming, just to gain friends, was giving in to peer pressure. Greg mastered the English language, graduated with honors and entered high school the next fall.

High school was like a brand new life beginning all over again for Greg. Within the walls of the school his love for music, art, stage, writing, and friends could be fulfilled. Musicals, yearbook, pep squad, honor society, plays, backdrops, posters, school newspapers, cartoons, a singing group and friends kept his flame burning day and night. He loved the life God had granted him to live.

In spite of a more-than-full school and work schedule, Greg always had time for little surprises for his family. There were secret notes, candlelight dinners, instant entertainment, hugs and lots of smiles. Inside, Greg was guided by a love and dedication for the One who allowed him to live. He wanted to do right and help others do the same.

It was this knowledge of God's love and His plan, Greg's love for people and his ability to create happiness in others, that helped him hold his head high in his last year of schooling, the last year of his life. He had many friends, because he was a friend. A few days before his death, on the way back from Mexico, he asked his mother to wheel him into the gift shop at the airport. There, in his ever-so-

Canby High School Singing Group

weakened condition, he picked out individual gifts for his friends. His love for others did not return empty. Throughout his entire battle with an uncontrollable cancer, the Lord was his Shepherd, friends his faithful servants and comforters, his family his fortress. He so much wanted to keep on giving; it was someone else's turn.

God could have ended Greg's life when miscarriage threatened and spared him the trials of pain, suffering and awareness of death. His family could have been sheltered from prolonged grief and the separation of a son they held and loved for almost nineteen years. God could also have allowed Greg's body to overcome the deadly sting of cancer. God had a reason for Greg's birth, a purpose in his short life, a plan in his death. Greg was born to live, and Greg was born to die. God's plan had reached its fulfillment. It was time for Greg to go home, home to the One who held the master plan.

"BORN TO LIVE, BORN TO DIE?"

Why was I born; that I could live?
Why did I live; that I could love?
Why did I love; that I could serve?
Why did I serve; that I could teach?
Why did I teach; that God could save?
Why did God save; that I might live?
Why was I born; that I might die?
Why did I die; that I might live?

Written July 29th, 1985, while driving home from Greg's grave.

1st Grade
Bern, Switzerland

2 years old
Zürich,
Switzerland

2

ON STAGE

written August 11, 1987

"GUESS WHAT, I'm a star!" Greg hollered, deliriously happy, as he ran up to the door of the school bus. "You know my friend?" he continued, barely catching his breath, "Well, he's sick, so the director asked me to take his part. It's great, I can't believe it." He paused a second to inhale then blurted, "I'd better go and get busy on my lines and songs." He turned and ran back toward the school.

Greg's mom, the bus driver, understood his elation wasn't because his friend was ill, for Greg's loyalty to his friends was the same as it was to his family and to God; he strove to put them first. His high-spirited reaction had only revealed an inside yearning he'd treasured since he was but a little boy, a fervent desire to be at a place he dearly loved — on stage.

High School Musical
Oklahoma!
Spring of 1981

The days that followed were hectic. Music from the record *Oklahoma!* pulsated through the floors and walls, shifting in the late evening hours from Greg's room to the downstairs garage. The concrete floor mystically transformed into a stage where Greg repeatedly tapped out a routine from one of the scenes.

Midnight oil burned often and Greg grew weary. A pain in his knee was brushed off as just an aftereffect of falling on that side during a scuffle scene in the musical. He didn't have time to see a doctor. His hours were filled not only with perfecting his lines and songs, but also his studies; he was an honor roll student. He devoted time, as well, to drawing and writing for the school newspaper. Much energy and pride went into the designing and painting of the musical's massive backdrop, so when Greg talked of being tired, he had every reason; he did too much.

Greg's mom attended all but one of *Oklahoma!*'s near-professional performances. Her thoughts had time to wander back to Greg's younger years in the land of snow-capped peaks, lush productive valleys and historical buildings that housed the arts of past centuries.

It was in Bern, Switzerland, that Greg asked if he could try out for a part in the production of the famous story, "The Brementown Musicians." which was to be presented by the City Theater. The story tells the adventures of three animals on their way to the city to become famous musicians. "Please," he begged, "even if I have to be the rooster." He was only seven years old, so his parents decided it was not yet time for Greg to go — on stage.

Entertainer
9 years old
Bern, Switzerland

She also remembered how his dad had built him and his siblings a large puppet stage. The apartment house basement became the theater, Greg the writer and director. Making others happy and seeing the children's faces light up was all the reward Greg needed to spur him on to new ideas, new shows. He organized a troupe of actors, "hiring" those his heart went out to, those who needed to feel important. One young boy had eye problems; another had a hair lip and cleft palate, causing him to speak with a lisp, and then there was a little girl. Her father, who was a well-known Bernese folksong writer and singer, had recently been killed in an auto accident on his way to a show. Greg was an entertainer with a heart. In his own mind he was already — on stage.

Later, in Oregon, Greg's weariness became chronic and the ache in his knee nearly unbearable; he finally agreed to see a doctor. A large bulge had formed on his left knee. After two false diagnoses, an orthopedic specialist found the enlargement to be osteogenic sarcoma, a deadly bone cancer that strikes children in the peak of their youth. Greg was six weeks away from his eighteenth birthday.

Summer was filled with radiation therapy, hospital visits and chemotherapy. His frail body fought bravely as the poisons were dripped, injected and radiated into it. He barely recovered after a near lethal dose of chemotherapy. As his soft, blond hair fell out in clumps and open sores filled his mouth and intestinal tract, he shed few tears, though deep inside his blue eyes, pain and humiliation could be seen. First a blond wig, then a reddish one covered his baldness. His friends engulfed him with love and concern. To them,

As a redhead in
"David and Lisa"
Fall of 1981

and to all others who asked how he was doing, his answer was always, "I'm fine."

The doctor scheduled the treatments so Greg could go to summer camp. Setting his crutches aside, Greg, weak and thin, set out to implant joy in the hearts of his fellow campers. Strenuous hours were invested in preparation for the talent show. His stunts and songs brought laughter, instilled courage and stimulated tears. Facing daunting obstacles, Greg pursued his desire to be— on stage.

Fall came and Greg entered school as a senior. In spite of nausea and other side effects of his treatment, Greg seldom missed a day of school. Flu season hit, and Greg was not spared. His white blood count tumbled, prohibiting chemotherapy, and the lesions in his lungs tripled. Surgery to replace Greg's cancer-riddled knee and leg bone was postponed. Greg turned this negative into a positive with, "If they aren't going to operate, maybe I can try out for the fall play." His wish again came true as he portrayed an inmate in the heartwarming story of young people in an institute for the emotionally disturbed, entitled *David and Lisa*. With a throbbing, bulging knee, Greg was in his element— on stage.

The following spring, six weeks before graduation, in his own room, Greg slipped tranquilly into an eternal peace, cradled by the supporting arms of his family. His battle with a deadly opponent had ended. Greg had won, just as he had set out to do. He was with God, never again to struggle for life. The life he now had would be without end.

Greg's father and uncle chose a beautiful, hand-carved, pine casket. It was transported to the family dwelling where it was lined with Greg's favorite things. Greg's older brother and brother-in-law used the family van to transport his body to the memorial service and later to the grave. These decisions would have been Greg's choices. As family members, fellow students and dear friends gathered in a simple memorial service for Greg, his uncles and friends directed hymns of praise to the One who had called Greg home, led prayers on behalf of those who remained behind, and spoke words of encouragement to all. A singing group, of which Greg had been a member, sang songs Greg would have requested. Greg's older brother rewrote and sang a song in memory of their friendship. It was a service Greg would have wanted, personal and filled with love. Greg's body rested in a closed casket surrounded by beautiful flowers and plants, in a place where he had spent hundreds of tireless hours making others happy, and where he wanted and loved to be most of all, in his high school auditorium— on stage.

On Stage
Canby High School
April 1982

3

FOR WHOM DO WE MOURN?

GRIEF: an intense emotional suffering caused by loss, disaster, misfortune, etc.; acute sorrow, deep sadness.

Grief is a reaction, both physical and psychological, to the loss of anything precious. In most cases it is united with the loss of a loved one, but losing material possessions, a job, or experiencing a broken promise may also trigger this reaction. Any of these can suddenly bring on the primary onset of grief. The grieving process goes through several stages and may take weeks, months or years. It is clearly personalized with each griever's name on his or her own design; no two experience grief the same. Some grievers could even be considered "recovering grievers" as long as they live. People walk through the steps in their own way depending on who their support group is, and whether or not God is the source of their strength and comfort. Grief is natural; it comes without an invitation.

To ignore this emotion is to hinder the healing. Suppression may help for the moment, but can prolong the pain leading to a draining of emotional and physical strength. Anger, depression, addiction, obsession and illness can erupt when grief is unresolved. Grief not dealt with will surface again and again until a solution is found.

When Greg complained of a painful knee, after having landed on it many times during the musical *Oklahoma!*, Greg's parents were sure it was because he was pushing his body to the limit. It wasn't until a few months later, and after several false diagnoses, that the family learned of Greg's serious problem. The moment Greg's mother picked up the phone and heard the orthopedic specialist say that Greg quite possibly had bone cancer, stage one of her grieving process began, that of shock.

Shock can engulf all thinking processes; it is like groping in the dark with no real sense of time or surroundings. Shock also can erase reality, possibly leading the griever into unwise decisions. During these critical times, those closest to the griever will be able to see things more clearly and can offer valuable help.

In Greg's case, a biopsy was performed, after which surgery was immediately scheduled. There was little time to ask questions, to think. Because of unavoidable obligations, Greg's family took turns accompanying him to his encounters with the unknown. A dear neighbor requested to be on the surgical team for the biopsy: a comfort immeasurable. Standing over Greg's bed after the surgery, Greg's mom watched as he peacefully slept. The serene atmosphere was suddenly interrupted by a doctor who wanted to speak to her in private. In a small, dimly lighted room he told her his suspicions were confirmed—Greg had osteosarcoma, the same disease a well-known politician's son had. Why was she told this? Was it to be comforting? It wasn't.

A feeling of numbness spread throughout the body of Greg's mother, then her nerves pricked and burned like a million lightening-ing bolts. She could not speak. She dropped her head to her chest and stared at the floor. No one was there to take her hand. No one's eyes were there to meet hers. There was no need to cry—tears were blocked anyway. It was totally silent. For a fleeting moment she thought it was just a bad dream and someone would surely say any minute, "Wake up, wake up," but no one spoke. She couldn't move; her body was experiencing the ravaging effects of shock, that sudden disturbance or agitation of the mind and emotions. When she was finally able to speak, she asked for something to calm her now quivering body, but no one seemed to be authorized to do so; she felt abandoned. How did she make phone calls to relay the diagnosis? She doesn't remember. Should she have taken someone with her that day? But, she didn't know!

Fortunately the body has been blessed with a built-in safety feature which allows it to shut down when dealing with traumatic happenings. This phase may last for hours or even days, depending on the person and the help available. The body and mind experience feelings of paralysis and helplessness. If allowed to go on too long, serious physical difficulties can develop. One can only hope for relief, because the pain can become unbearable. For Greg's family it was a time of soul-searching, a time of asking, "What happened? What is bone cancer and why did Greg get it?" Was it a time to give up, or was it a time to pick up the scattered pieces and try to make some clear picture out of them? God already had.

Once a person is rescued from shock, another phase in the grieving process takes occupancy. This is a period of emotional responses to the loss. For Greg's mother, the second stage meshed with the first. Deep darkness, physical weakness, fear and questions such as, "Could this have been prevented?" or "What can be done now?" tore into diminishing reserves. The future had no meaning, the past was gone; days were long, nights were longer. It was as if the curtain had just come down after the last act of a play, but there was no applause. Everything was still. Was someone out there? Who would be the first to speak? What was there to say? Why was it so dark? Where was the light? Tears flowed easily and often.

The shedding of tears is known to be a very important part of the grief-healing process. Tears help those in grief to work through intense feelings and guide their emotions into an awareness that aids in healing. Tears should not be associated with weakness or losing control, but rather as self-help, a God-given self-help. The Lord tells us to weep with those who weep. He himself wept.

Yes, many begin their grieving process from the moment they are informed of their loved one's hopeless state, while others prefer to put reality aside and cling to a ray of hope they have created in their hearts. All are, in their own ways, preparing for the moment of a final separation. God determines the time. Some are given days, months or even years to support and care for their loved ones. It is almost like being allowed to say a slow good-bye. Even if not spoken, thoughts of death, memorial services and family creep in during this prolonged time. These thoughts can be viewed as a positive step in coping.

Sometimes a phone call or a knock on the door can bring one into immediate confrontation with death; no warning, no forethought, no preparation time, just an abrupt separation from a loved one. Shock enters and the grief-stricken must face innumerable responsibilities that can tax even the strongest. Time is not granted to work slowly through the phases of grief, because grief can actually be put on hold by shock. There will be a pattern for these grievers as there is for all in sorrow. Relief and refuge are nigh—God knows.

Some in sorrow have a deep need to verbally go over and over the cause of their grief. Others pen their feelings. Some do both. A few remain silent. Then there are those who can close the chapter and move on. Almost immediately they begin removing belongings of the deceased, change the room and begin anew. They may be seeking to take away any daily reminders of what once was and now is gone. Others don't want anything disturbed for a time. For them, just touching things once worn or cherished by their loved one can bring about new eruptions of grief. Some make the deceased's room available to those who wish to reminisce, look at pictures, touch memories or grieve. Then there are a few cases where the room is turned into a shrine, as if the loved one will one day return.

Most, however, are able to eventually take on the task of sorting through all the memories. Though some prefer to walk this memory lane alone, others reach out for help from those who have demonstrated love, patience and empathy. Certain bends in the road can be very difficult. Forcing time limits or even decisions upon grievers as they sort through keepsakes only prolongs their recovery and can also bring about frustration and relapse. It is a day-by-day working through, a time of reflection and a time of self-examination. One day may go well, while the following few may seem like a sliding backwards, starting back on square one. These important steps do eventually lead through the valley and on to higher ground.

Each griever knows when the time is right to take the next step. At first, grief is like a sea of scattered pieces, a puzzle with not even so much as a border with which to begin. Then slowly, one by one, the pieces begin to fit into each other. Often when least expected, the unknown transforms into a distinctly clear picture. This welcomed relief, this feeling of a weight being lifted, is brought about by facing reality, by allowing oneself to accept the outcome as God's will, God's plan for the griever. It is this resignation that erases the destructive forces of anger, doubt and fear. The "whys" are slowly replaced with, "I think I now understand," and the countenance is gently lifted to view the future.

It seems it is not so much how, when, where or why the grieving takes place, but the attitude of the heart that either makes or breaks the one in grief. It is this attitude also that God looks upon and it is this attitude that those around the griever look upon. God has not promised an easy walk through the valley, but He has promised help to those who ask. He can then use this opportunity to teach, comfort and strengthen the faith of the distressed one, as well as those looking on. God is able to turn the negative into positive, sadness into joy and allow the sun to appear from behind the dark clouds. These rays of hope inspire recovery.

❖

The bees sip the honey from the clover
      surrounding Greg's grave;
    They have come here the past nine years
      to sip and to save.

God created them as he did our son,
      with a purpose, a goal;
    But God gave Greg something special,
      a living soul.

A small squirrel from the woods creeps toward me,
      not shy;
    Near the grave he staggers, gasps for air,
      lies down to die.

None of God's creation can know
      the length of their duty here;
    God alone keeps the list, for us a mystery,
      for Him it is clear.

Not even a sparrow is unaccounted for,
      God knows each one;
    His love is endless, for you, for me,
      and for my son.

No, I don't always understand every feeling,
      renewed eruptions of pain;
    God promises me comfort though,
      knowing I will see Greg again.

It is with this hope of spending eternity
      with those who have gone on before,
    That I greet each day knowing God
      has something better for me in store.

So on this earth I must stay, at least for today,
    or for the time God gives;
  Then with my son, I will go to the One
    whose promise forever lives.

Help me, God, to keep the faith,
    stay strong during the length of my stay;
  Knowing as Greg was called, so must I,
    prepare me for that day.

Recovery is a regaining of balance, control, composure or the retrieval of something that was lost. It is to get back on one's feet after having sorted through the many chambers of the heart. This is the time the griever has hoped for, prayed for; it is a time to face the challenges with confidence, knowing God is close at hand and comforters are standing ready.

Recovery puts the griever in an active role. Earlier phases entered the scene with little or no prompting; their roles were passive. Coping, accepting, smiling, and then restoring an interest in life are now within reach and the picture becomes even more complete. Recovery, however, can be greatly hindered when a griever feels that letting go, even just a little, would be like a betrayal of the deceased loved one. More time is then needed to stop and evaluate before recovery can continue. As soon as the loss is accepted, doors open and the path, once darkened, will be lighted. The Lord is the Light and the Way. He will help bear the load, ease the pain, and bring about an understanding of the difficulties. God will make those in grief whole again and will allow them to see His plan and purpose for their walk through the valley.

The recovery stage was a very, very long process for the mother of Greg. There was no explanation for the years it would take to work through her feelings of grief. Her case would fall into the category of a lifelong, recovering griever. She had told Greg good-bye the night she felt him take his last breath in her arms, and enough time had passed to bring about healing, according to those who specialize in the grieving process. Accepting the loss as God's will was never doubted. She believed Greg's death was a decision God had made out of love, for God is Love. Then what was the reason for her continuous grief? Was she seeking God's reassurance or was it the course designed for her?

Greg's father bore his grief silently, remaining strong for the family and others, relieving them of responsibilities so they could administer to Greg's needs. He seldom revealed his emotions. As a spiritual leader he accepted God's will and looked to the future, not to the past. He, seemingly, passed quickly from one period of grief to the next, entering the recovery stage ahead of most of the family. It was his way and God knew the role he needed to play.

All of Greg's siblings had played an intimate part in his life; he had taken time for each one of them. Before Greg became ill the family had adopted a brother and sister pair from abroad. These children fit in the middle of the other five, so Greg's sibling support group then numbered seven. They all bore various levels grief because they had lost one of their best friends, the one who had entertained them, played with them and comforted them when they were down and out. How could they go on without him?

For Greg's brothers and sisters there would be a vacant chair at the table where Greg kept everyone in suspense with his stories. Would anyone even know what to say without Greg being there? His room upstairs would be empty and his voice would no longer be heard through the walls as he rehearsed lines or songs for the school productions. He would not be found in the same place at his desk when they needed quick help with a drawing, an art project or a great idea for a surprise for one of their friends. Greg's days of dressing up and scaring them were over as were the fun and games in the upper hallway. Who would hold the door shut and say, "Just try to tag me." His "Hi, I'm home," and his quick footsteps on the stairs would be missed. The shuffling about in the room above the kitchen would cease. An emptiness entered the house. No one ever thought about rehearsing what he or she would do or say when

Greg would no longer be with them as a very integral part of their everyday lives. They didn't want him to go. They thought he would get well. They were lost without him. They missed him.

Just as everyone had found a new place in the family when the adopted children came, so would they again have to shift places now that their brother's place was empty. Slowly each one began adjusting, seeking a spot that gave them new security. Their hearts became storage places for the uncountable memories—memories of their own Greg, the Greg they knew in a way no other one of them could. Some of these memories then, somehow, worked their way to the surface in each of the children in little, indescribable ways, allowing Greg to live on in them. God knew.

Many years later, Greg's father was asked to write the following article on the pain of losing a child.

Death is not a friend and was never meant to be (1 Cor. 15:26). The burden it imposes upon a family's soul is difficult to measure. Especially onerous is the death of one's child. As some of us know firsthand, the pain lingers deep and long. Understanding this, Jesus was not unmoved by the sight of a widowed mother accompanying her only son to his burial. He well knew that for her difficult times lay ahead and "He felt compassion for her" (Luke 7:13).

It is not uncommon for parents to become angry over the loss of a child. When they contemplate their investment, their unfulfilled dreams, and the curtailment of their joy, the perceived injustice fills them with indignation.

The temptation to get mad at God also lingers near. How well Job understood this. When he received news of the simultaneous and violent death of his ten children, for whom he had been so solicitous before God in life (Job 1:2, 4–5,18–19), Job spontaneously fell to the ground to worship his creator (Job 1:20). "The Lord gave and the Lord has taken away, blessed be the name of the Lord. Through all this Job did not sin nor did he blame God" (Job 1:21–22).

Often, feelings of guilt mingle with anger. In Elijah's flight from wicked Jezebel, the prophet came to dwell in the home of a widow in the Sidonean village Zarephath (1Kings 17:9–16). During Elijah's stay there, the widow's son fell ill and died. Responding aggressively to her heartrending loss, the widow turned to Elijah, saying, "What do I have to do with you, O man of God, you have come to me to bring my iniquity to remembrance and to put my son to death" (1 Kings 17:18). Not unlike many others before and after, this widow viewed her son's death as God's punishment for her past sins. Just how baseless her assumption was, is evidenced by the subsequent resurrection of the child from the dead (1 Kings 17:19–23).

Almost without exception, bereaved parents are also assaulted by a vicious void, a profound sense of loneliness. News of the death of even a murderously rebellious son can break a parent's heart. It did in David's case. Although he had barely escaped death at the hands of his treasonous son, David's heart still convulsed with pain upon that son's less than honorable demise. "Oh my son Absalom, my son, my son Absalom. Would I had died instead of you, O Absalom my son, my son" (2 Sam. 18:33).

How attached we become to our children! And rightly so. God is attached to His children, too. But how do we deal with their death? Can life be worth living after such a loss? Can there still be joy? Yes, in Christ there can be, indeed there must be (Phil. 4:4)! As in every frustrating turn of events, we need understanding of God and of His ways in order to successfully deal with the stress and challenge of a child's death.

God is love (1 John 4:8), and He loves every child born to man and acts in their best interest (cf. Jonah 4:11; John 3:16). Surely, we have no right to demand children, nor can we create them ourselves. They are God's "gift" to us and are intended by Him to bless us (Psalm 127:3–5). In "giving" us children, however, God does not relinquish His own claim upon them. They are first and foremost His children, ours only to prepare for a return to Him (Eph. 6:4). In effect then, children are merely "on loan" from God; His claim upon them far exceeds that of all earthly parents. We do well not to lose sight of this fact.

When God allows our child to die, we may not assume to know why. Job didn't. It was not heaven's will to let this God-fearing father know why he suddenly suffered the loss of his children. God simply expected Job to trust divine wisdom's ability to properly operate the universe. Confronted with just a few questions about how this world and its inhabitants function, any desire which Job may have had to challenge God's sovereign rule suddenly left him (Job 44:35, 42:1–6).

Not only may we count on God's wisdom and power, but we may also reckon with His care. Our pain He understands quite well. After all, He suffered the death of His Son, too. "He who did not spare His own Son, but delivered Him up for us all, how will He not also with Him freely give us all things?" (Rom. 8:32).

That surely includes comfort and strength to deal triumphantly with the death of a child (cf. Rom. 8:35–39). And that is cause for joy (Jas. 1:2).

Comforters Welcome

The role of a comforter often comes without warning, invitation or an instruction booklet. Because a griever needs individual consideration, comforters must carefully and patiently try to understand this uniqueness. It does not take a degree in counseling, but rather a heart full of love and compassion to be qualified for this most important role. Neither does it require a special vocabulary, because silence may be best. A touch on the hand, a squeeze of the arm or a hug are unspoken ways to reach out. Also eye contact allows the griever and the comforter to see into each other's heart. A few chosen words may be needed to open a verbal channel of communication. Good listening skills will be honored. Words put in writing and given or mailed can then be read over and over again, each time reminding the griever that someone cares.

Comforters may stay on standby, ready when needed. Some who mourn will not reach out for comfort; others will. Sensitivity and insight are worthy tools in making decisions to help. Doing something, even if it doesn't come out perfectly, evidences love and concern. Doing nothing shows lack of both. Those who experience a loss generally receive attention for the first few days or even weeks, then it begins to dwindle. Comforters may begin to wonder if their services are still welcome. A phone call or a short visit will confirm just where the griever may be in terms of coping with their loss.

Notes and letters will remain a very important means of comfort in the months and years ahead. Receiving kind thoughts, even many years later, will bring an indescribable message of love. Grief can be compared to a wound; some heal over quickly, others take longer. Then there are those which heal but leave painful scars. True comforters are like a soothing balm to any wound and can also help in the fading away of unpleasant scars. Because their role in a griever's life is necessary and so very valuable, comforters need to be encouraged to seek every opportunity to serve. It may, at times, be difficult to actually walk in the shoes of those in mourning, but it will be possible to walk alongside.

❖

Help Me to Walk in Your Shoes

I understand,
       I know just how you must feel;
It took my son Greg's death
       to make it all real.

For years I thought I understood,
       I thought I knew;
Like the day I came with open arms
       to comfort you.

I tried within to imagine
       just how it would be,
If a child of mine were to be taken
       away from me.

Deeply I searched for words,
       the right things to say,
I felt, just maybe,
       I might take some of the pain away.

But your eyes revealed something
       I didn't quite understand;
Your body seemed weary
       as I reached for your hand.

It was a language so foreign;
       I felt somewhat lost;
I wanted to learn, what would it take;
       what was the cost?

You needed someone who understood,
        had been there like you.
I looked around, I was made aware,
        true comforters were few.

That night I prayed for wisdom,
        to show me a way in due time;
To be able to slip into your shoes
        and make your feelings mine.

The time then came too quickly,
        the course was offered and yet,
The curriculum was overwhelming;
        would I willingly accept?

As I sit at Greg's grave, alone,
        on this beautiful spring day;
I am assured God's plan was fulfilled
        so I can truly say:

I understand,
        I know now just how you must feel;
It took my son Greg's death
        to make it all real.

May I use every crossing of a bridge,
        each scaling of a wall and every finishing of a race,
To help me put one of my feet, if not two,
        in your shoes and let God set our pace.

II

WRITINGS

A.

WRITINGS OF GREG'S MOTHER

4

MY GOD AND I

THE FOLLOWING are writings by Greg's mother. They are not written sitting at a desk or table with pen and ink, but written from wherever her heart carried her — no boundaries, no set times or places, just a place where she could record the ever-pounding emotions of the heart.

God and I have many meeting places. They are open to me each day from morning until night. Some of these meeting places were very special during Greg's battle with cancer.

Each night after Greg would hobble out to get washed up for bed, I would straighten his bed, fluff his pillow and open the window to allow fresh night air into his somewhat isolated room. As I viewed the Big Dipper along with all of the stars I would talk to God and ask Him to watch over Greg for the night. We loved him so.

All along the freeway from our house to the clinic in Portland, sometimes twice a day, I would talk, pray and sing. My favorite song was, "I Know that My Redeemer Lives." God knew how difficult those last few curves were, how the tears began to flow before I reached the top of the hill. When a motorcycle policeman stopped me for going too fast in the curves, God is the only One who understood why I sobbed uncontrollably, while the compassionate officer looked helpless. God knew I wanted to be strong for Greg. We talked about it often.

On my knees, in the darkness of the small master bathroom, I could pour out my entire heart to God. There we could meet alone in the quietness of the hour. Just God and I were up.

On the couch in the downstairs living room, gazing out into the night as all above were sleeping, I would feel the closeness of God and His creation. This was one of my favorite, most frequently visited meeting places.

In the last days of Greg's life I especially felt the nearness of God as I sat on the floor beside his bed while he slept. I received comfort from the Master Comforter as I poured out my heart. God was such a close part of our relationship and this place of meeting seemed so right.

After Greg's death God and I often met as I was driving the school bus trying to keep my thoughts on the road and my job. Memories of Greg kept creeping in at every turn and at every stop at the schools. This was his town, his life.

Probably the most frequent place I continually meet with God is Greg's grave. It is here in solitude that I can put aside all of this world's interruptions and feel totally alone with the One whose love for Greg, and for me, is endless.

1982

May 30ᵗʰ, 1982

Determined to overcome grief, Greg's father and mother chose to attend the senior awards assembly, the assembly Greg had looked forward to with expectations. Parents strained to locate their sons or daughters in the crowd as they entered the auditorium and found their seats. Greg's mother couldn't lift her eyes and wished she hadn't come; tears flowed. She was overcome with sorrow. Greg's father comforted her as he solemnly watched the procession.

After what seemed like hours, the audience was asked to rise and stand in silent reverence for Greg Earnhart, a member of their graduating class who was no longer with them. Greg's younger brother was then called upon to step forward. With tears flowing down his cheeks, he graciously accepted Greg's graduation cap and then the honors Greg had earned through much hard work. These awards now rest in a bookcase in Greg's home; in time they will perish. More important are the memories of Greg's life, a life in which he sought to honor God.

❖

June 30th, 1982
in the living room at home

Every day there are fragrances, times,
        objects and moods.

There are atmospheres, clothing
        and music.

There are foods, cards, letters,
        rooms and prayers.

There are streets, places, voices.

There are people, feelings, words
        and thoughts.

And there are dreams.

They are all a part of Greg and
        I miss him.

❖

July 21ˢᵗ, 1982

in the living room at home three months after Greg's death.

Oh, God, why did You call Greg so soon,
        just when he became a man
        and could go out on his own;
    why was he ever born,
    only to leave in such short time?

Just when we could finally talk
        and we were finding each other's hearts.

Just when he had dedicated himself to Thee,
    his heart, his soul, his all.

Just when he was about to graduate with honors,
        scholarships, awards.

Just when the future stood like a sea of dreams,
        only to reach for one.

Just when we finally felt
    we could allow the world to test him.

Just when relationships
    were rewarding and fulfilling.

Just when he allowed himself
    to open the doors of his heart and reveal his life.

Is it because —
    He can serve You better in death than in life?

    Or because he had had such a struggle in his short life
        and You wanted him to be at peace?

Did You want him to be an example to others in
    suffering?
Or maybe —
    Yes, I know I needed to learn so many things too,
        like what really is important and what isn't,
        or what it means to lose someone
        who is a part of your very being.

    Oh, how often have I thought of You and Your Son,
        how You had to watch Him suffer and die.
        I knew You understood how I felt.
        I begged that You allow my son to live,
        but asked also,
        that I be willing to give him to You if it would be
        to Your honor and glory,
        to the saving of his soul and the souls of others.

    Do I need to realize that little problems, illnesses and
        trials are so trivial and that life is so precious?

    Also that life here is a vapor or a pilgrimage and
        gathering treasures for the wandering is worthless?

But,
    Now God, where do I find the middle way,
        not to give up and want to be with Greg on
        one hand, and on the other not to put all my
        effort into gaining rewards here?

    How much do I need to exist and serve Thee,
        not to look back nor to store for the future?

Oh,
    God, help me!

1983

(1 Year)

March 4ᵗʰ, 1983

in the living room at home

All day I wanted to go to Greg's grave, but there was no time. Guests filled our house prior to attending the high school musical. Watching three of Greg's brothers perform on stage with another one co-directing, brought memories of Greg and his love for the stage.

At home after the family went upstairs to bed, I was alone with my thoughts and feelings. Actually, I wanted to leave, go away. Instead I dressed warm and went outside in the cool still night. I sat on the ground beside the tree that was planted in memory of Greg. The dogwood tree was in full bloom, fresh and alive. There I stayed for a long time, telling God, the only One who really understands my heart, about what was inside of me.

When Greg was so ill, God and I would talk for hours and hours. I received inner strength from Him to go on another day and then another. Tonight as I gaze into the heavens and talk to my Creator I feel inadequate and now know that without Him I would be lost. It is at times like tonight that my whole life parades before me and I see the worthlessness of things in this world; they will fade and die. Only our souls will stand before God, alone. When will this be? Will God be gracious? I pray He will allow me to join the saved.

I continue writing this now on the hearth by candlelight after having come in from outside. It seems it has only been a few nights ago that I was down here begging God to spare Greg's life. God knew what Greg needed and what I needed. I do not know what God has in store for me tomorrow. I do pray I can accept it with courage and in doing so glorify and honor His name. Goodnight.

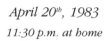

April 20ᵗʰ, 1983
11:30 p.m. at home

It was about this time a year ago they carried Greg's body away. His struggle was over. We had lost a son; God had taken him home. There was a great feeling of sadness and loss. Tonight the feeling is the same as I sit here alone in the living room; the family upstairs sleeps.

I want to leave, just get away for a while with my thoughts. As I quietly open the front door I pause on the front porch to listen to the night creatures. The air smells cool and fresh as I look up toward heaven, the place my heart reaches out to as I talk to God. Both cats crawl into my lap and keep me warm as I sit on the porch, as if to say, "We will make you feel better." Beside me is the dogwood tree that was given to us by the drama club in Greg's memory. Its soft pink blossoms glow in the tiny rays of light from the street lamp.

I'm wondering if I'll ever be able to overcome these feelings of loss; why must I continue to be so sad? God knows my very being, my inner struggles. He has been merciful and good.

I must go inside now and try to sleep. Goodnight.

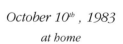

October 10ᵗʰ , 1983
at home

I had a dream the other night that Greg came home to visit us. He was blond, pale, but warm and sweet. As he came in and hugged me so tenderly; his dad was nearby and said in a kind voice, "Greg, you must go now; it is too hard on your mom." I woke up feeling confused, knowing it was only a dream revealing the deep feelings of my heart, wanting to see Greg again, but it was just a dream.

1984

(2 Years)

February 1ˢᵗ, 1984
at home

This is a day I seem to have lived before. It is a day I didn't think I would have to live again. Our youngest son, eight years younger than Greg, has a tumor behind his knee. The place of the tumor is almost the same as Greg's was, only the opposite leg. Symptoms are the same, feelings identical. Greg's brother is barely twelve. The first diagnosis is "osteochondriosome," meaning bone plus cartilage. The base of the tumor is about the size of a half-dollar.

Because of two false diagnoses with Greg's illness, we decided to seek more opinions including two prominent bone specialists, our own pediatrician, a top bone surgeon, a naturopath and a medical clinic in Mexico. Surgery was set for March 6th and the film kept playing before my eyes.

I wanted to hear the report, but again I didn't. The doctor entered smiling and gave us the good news: no cancer. The shaking inside became worse because of deep relief, and then I wanted to cry. Our young son knew little about what was taking place in our hearts. He was, however, aware of what had taken the life of his brother and surely had his own concerns. Even though the danger of cancer was erased, Greg's brother remained fearful of the dreaded disease.

All afternoon as I drove the school bus up and down through our little town my thoughts were a prayer to God in deep thanksgiving for His mercy and grace.

1985

(3 Years)

March 14ᵗʰ, 1985
at home

Today I was at the bedside of a 15-year-old boy with cancer. Ever since he first stepped into my school bus, several years ago, he has reminded me of Greg. Like Greg, he is light-skinned, frail, and says, "I'm fine" when asked how he is doing. As yet he doesn't know about Greg, but he must sense my desire to be there for him. He is in stage four, after extended chemotherapy, tests and surgery. It is hard, but I want to try to help this young man with the understanding God has allowed me to experience. As he is my last student off in the afternoon I have been given permission to pull the bus over, park it and listen to whatever is in his heart. There is a bond and I think I need him as much as he might need me. He is a positive fighter; he shows his strength as he daily overcomes many odds.

April 21ˢᵗ, 1985

Three years ago tonight almost to the hour Greg parted from this world to be with his Maker forever. How well I recall his last breaths, with long pauses in-between, then complete silence and it was over. My feelings inside are the same tonight as they were three years ago: deep, unbearable grief and pain.

I don't know why this last week has been so hard for me. No one really knows about my tears or the inner poundings of loneliness. I carry them alone with God. I talk to Him a lot and He gives me new strength and composure to make it just a few more hours. The pain is, most of the time, somewhat easier to bear than it was even last year, or six months ago, but it is still there. God most certainly understands, having a Son who died a very devastating death. God is so gracious to me.

Today our oldest son was asked to lead a song because the song leader was late. He quickly picked, "The Lord is my Shepherd," the Psalm I read to Greg minutes before he passed into eternal sleep. The evening assembly was devoted to a report on his dad's preaching trip to Germany where the balance of Greg's memorial fund was sent for the work there. Greg's heart was always in part abroad, where he was born and where he hoped to someday return, possibly to teach others the gospel. It was hard to cover the emotions even at home when we later had a house full of guests. After they left and all the family had been tucked in bed, I came here to the church building to write, where the only noises are the creaks from the old structure and squeaks from the wind turbines on the roof. God is my Guide. Without Him I would never be able to get up each new morning. May God never forsake me and may I always remain faithful.

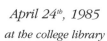

April 24ᵗʰ, 1985
at the college library

I am sitting in the college library having been able to ride up with Greg's younger brother who is here in school. I am trying to write some thoughts about Greg, but it is very difficult. I must remain composed and shed only quiet tears; there are many others here studying. It was just three years ago today that Greg's body was laid to rest in the cemetery in Salem. It is so very difficult, but I must try to do what I came here to do.

❖

June 23ʳᵈ, 1985
in the berry field

The scent of strawberries surrounds me and the children in the fields. The hot breeze of the late June warms my body. Uncountable times a day tingling feelings inside erupt and then subside. Not even berry stains on my hands and clothes can distract me from reliving what happened almost exactly four years ago.

It was during berry season in 1981 that Greg was diagnosed as having bone cancer. This report opened up a whole new chapter in our lives. We thought we had, in nearly a half century on this earth, experienced almost everything at least once. Soon, however, all of our senses were entering a new training school. Unknown feelings were confronting us every day, if not every minute. The most difficult part of the schooling was that of making decisions in areas totally foreign to us. Now it only takes one scent, face, situation, atmosphere or time of year to open up a bottomless crater of emotions. When will there be a reprieve? Together with God I have come this far and each new day will also be in His hands.

❖

June 9ᵗʰ, 1985
at home

Today I spent the noon hour with the young man who has cancer. He is on oxygen. He is brave.

I also received a note from a mother whose boy was killed a year ago. I had written her knowing how hard it still was for her. She said, "We miss him so much;" how well I know.

❖

July 29ᵗʰ, 1985
in the car while driving home from the grave

Why was I born, that I could live?
Why did I live, that I could love?
Why did I love, that I could serve?
Why did I serve, that I could teach?
Why did I teach, that God could save?
Why does God save, that I might live?
Why was I born, that I might die?
Why did I die, that I might live?

❖

October 10ᵗʰ, 1985
at home

A brother of one of our son's friends died in a tragic home accident.

We went immediately to visit. Through hugs and tears the mom said, "I know you understand."

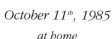

October 11ᵗʰ, 1985
at home

We went to a funeral of an older boy who died of a freak accident after he had survived surgery for a brain tumor. His mom works in the high school office and was a great comfort to us during Greg's illness. She, too, knew we understood.

Understanding the death of a child in the truest sense comes only after having experienced it personally. I did not understand it before; I do now, and there is a reason I needed to understand.

❖

December 7ᵗʰ, 1985
at home

Tonight Greg's younger brother called from college in the Southeast. He is due home in a few weeks for the holidays. He said, "I think I need to have my blood checked. I have been dizzy again and weak. Also my body doesn't heal fast when I get a cut or bruise." My heart ached, my insides burned and my body trembled.

I said to myself, "Oh, son, why did you tell me? Why must I know? Why must you fear and why must I fear? Oh, son, I don't like these feelings. I can't sleep; problems overcome me. I go downstairs to the same place I always went to pray when Greg was so ill. God is the only One who really understands.

"Oh, God please spare this son the fear, the sorrow, the pain, the separation that a dreaded disease brings with it. Allow him, dear Lord, to grow up, to be a faithful servant of Thine, to experience the love and joy of his own family, to have a job and share with others the many blessings he has received from Thee. Help him to honor Thy Name in all things, if it be Thy will, Oh, God."

1986
(4 Years)

February 22ⁿᵈ, 1986
at home

Today I was made to think of Greg so many times as my temperature climbed up over 103 degrees. My body neared uselessness and my strength diminished. Now I know why Greg often didn't feel like smiling or talking. He never found relief as I did when my fever broke and I slowly recovered. Greg's relief came in death, not before. Greg never wanted to be a burden to anyone, so he kept a lot of feelings inside.

I can now in some small way better understand what Greg went through; it must have been unbearable.

August 19ᵗʰ, 1986
at home

Last night I dreamed of Greg. I was almost afraid to look at him, afraid I wouldn't know him, but he looked the same, even younger, healthy and pink-cheeked. He leaned over to me, almost touched my cheek, and said, "Everything is OK, just one spot on my chest won't heal." He then left and I woke up.

1987
(5 Years)

May 24ᵗʰ, 1987
at home

A dream of Greg

He so wanted to come home. His younger brother saw him, we all saw him and he was coming home to share a room with his little brother. We were so happy to have him home again. We didn't know how it was possible, but we knew it was time. I talked to him and he was coming home. He wasn't sick anymore; he was well and looked so good.

5

THE PATH TO THE GRAVEYARD

*A step-by-step look at what takes place
when this mother visits the grave of her son.*

The
Setting

A T HOME, as she fills in her new calendar for the year, she writes in her son's birthday, as she does for all the others. She finds the day of his death and marks that as well. These are two special times she plans to visit the grave.

On these special days she gathers a blanket, flat pillow, jacket, hat and umbrella, depending on the weather. Also she takes pencils (easy to erase), paper (spiral notebook is ideal), Kleenex and a hard surface to write on. Last, but not least, she walks around the outside of the house before she leaves, carefully selecting flowers in season and greenery. These are placed in a jar or in a very wet towel to stay fresh.

The drive to the cemetery takes about 35 minutes, so there is time to let the heart prepare for the day. As the car nears the gate of the graveyard, her eyes already swell with tears as if it were the very first visit. Through the gate she slowly comes to a stop, gets out and selects a grave vase from a pile of other green, coned-shaped vases. Now, she very slowly turns down an incline to the edge of the graves and parks out of the way.

With all things in hand, she first crosses the road to pause for a moment at the grave of her dearest friend. It was through this friend and her family that she had learned about God and His plan for her soul. From childhood she and her friend had planned to grow old together, but God had other plans.

Crossing back over the road, just a few graves below her son's, she kneels beside the place where her mother was buried in 1976 at the age of 71. She reflects for a moment on an 18-year old girl who immigrated to America with only a fourth grade education and how she became a mother, only to be left alone with her children. Her positive, "Where there is a will, there is a way," carried them all through tough times. This self-assured attitude is evident in her family; yes, it was also in her young grandson who is buried just above her on the slope.

After about ten steps, she places her pillow, along with the other things, at the edge of the stone with her son's name on it. A couple of steps away is a water faucet where she fills the grave vase and arranges the flowers before she pushes it into the ground at the edge of the gravestone. She reads the inscription on the grave as if it is the very first time — tears swell and memories rush into the soul like a powerful ocean tide. She begins to write without forethought; the heart provides the words. Later her poetry emerges unexpectedly; it has to be this way.

Gregory
Dean
Earnhart

1983

(1 Year)

Place of
Prayer

❖

April 15ᵗʰ, 1983

The beautifully carved stone I am looking at has the name Gregory Dean Earnhart engraved deep into its surface. It is the name we chose with pride some 20 years ago for our new son. On this crisp sunny day I sit alone on the side of this hill, looking over a vast green lawn scattered with bunches of flowers lovingly placed at graves here and there. The breeze touches the trees. My God knows I am here. He knows my heart is heavy, for only a year ago the very place I am sitting was just another piece of lawn. Now there is a stone, and my son Greg's body lies beneath it.

My tears make it difficult to write. I have placed a small plant on the grave, not for Greg, for he is not here. I bring flowers because that is what he would do for someone he loved. He would even be here with me, comforting me. He would recall the good times and tell me to remember all the exciting things we did together. Greg would not want me to be sad, but would tell me to think about being able to see him again where we will never have to leave each other. He always had a soft touch for those in sorrow, so I, too, am comforted knowing what he would do. Thank you, Greg, for the example you set and for your sincere love for others.

I didn't know my faith had to be tested or my sincerity tried, but God knew what I needed in order to be aware of His requirements. Would a curable disease have had such a lasting effect? Once Greg was well, would I have forgotten the trying times? Greg once said, "Mom, I don't think a broken leg would have made me turn completely to God. It had to be something more." He went on to say, "I know how much God loves me and wants to save my soul." God was always a part of Greg's life.

It is hard to give up a child. God knows this best of all as "He gave His only begotten Son, that those who believe in Him would have eternal life." God's plan is to save souls, not lives.

No one seemed to love life and its beauty more than Greg. He expressed it, showed it, wrote about it, helped others to find love and happiness; yet, in the end, as life's flame slowly went out, he did not complain. He was prepared to meet God, even though he so much wanted to live.

As I sit here, I am made to think back a year when we all gathered here to see where Greg's body would lie. So many came to comfort us. Greg's ten-year-old little brother paused as we started to walk away from the casket, not wanting to leave his brother. Two of Greg's closest friends laid a pink flower on the casket. Pink was the color they used to tease each other; it was their last goodbye. Comfort surrounded us.

For today, I must leave. I will stop again by my mother's grave. Her stone says, "Dorothy Wellbrock 1905–1976." My mother was in Switzerland when Greg was born — she held him; she loved him.

❖

July 29th, 1983

It was 20 years ago today that God gave us Greg. I am here at the grave, not because I know Greg is here, but because I can be alone with my thoughts and tears; they flow in one constant stream, dampening my writing pad.

Why do I keep coming here? I do not know why. I do know Greg would be here at the grave of someone he loved if that some-one had a birthday. After having given Greg gifts and surprises for 18 years, it wasn't possible to pass up this day without some small token of my love. This little feathery bird will sit by the stone until the caretaker grooms the grass again. Greg had a way of making birthdays so very special for those he loved. Today there is no one to help me celebrate except the birds, the sun and the beautiful trees; but we are not alone. God, the One who has called Greg home to be His son, is here, and I thank Him.

My heart yearns for the time I can be with Greg again, know-ing God's promises will erase whatever lack of understanding I might now feel. There will be no more tear-smeared pages, no more leaving those you love and no more heavy hearts. It is by faith I believe this; otherwise, I could not bear another day. This same faith allows me to know that Greg is safe, secure and at peace with God. May the glory go to Him who created Greg for a purpose, and there-after, called him home to rest.

To children of God, death, as well as life, has a meaning even if at times we fail to see it. It is motherly to want to keep your children near you forever. God, too, wants His children near Him, knowing they are then secure. Never again can anything harm, tempt or hurt them.

As I sit here today, after caring for my very dearest friend who has cancer, many thoughts have crossed my mind. Sitting close to her, listening to her difficult breathing and feeling her weak body reminded me often of the courageous battle Greg had fought. She is in God's hands; her hour is near. It is hard at times to bear the pain again, but she needs me and I need her. God will help. She will be called to cross over, just as each of us will be called. When and how this crossing takes place makes no real difference. The important factor is that we are prepared to cross. God helped Greg to the other side. He will help my friend and each of us.

It is getting cool here at the grave. Two elderly gentlemen have come to rearrange flowers on a grave. I will leave for now, but if God wills, I shall return.

1984

(2 Years)

April 17ᵗʰ, 1984

It is April. Two years ago, Greg was relieved of his struggles and pain to go in peace to his Creator and Savior.

The gravesite today looks a little weather-beaten from the many winter rains, but Greg's name stands bold and beautiful, bringing back memories of when he was born. I had always wanted a Greg. Now Greg's older brother has asked for the privilege to use Greg's full name for a son of his, if the Lord were to bless him with a son. I was touched.

It is somewhat cool today; the sun hides at times behind massive clouds. When it does peek through, it paints a backdrop of warm, exotic pastels on the spring trees, shrubs and flowers.

Two new grave plots have been prepared for services here today for those whose walk on this earth has ended. The white hearse passes with a dozen cars close behind. Were these people as blessed as Greg to die in the Lord? Were they prepared to meet their God? Did they too want to live and serve God as much as Greg wished? For them it is too late to even regard such questions; their lot has been cast and eternity has begun.

For us who are still pilgrims on this earth, we must also ask ourselves if we are prepared for this day, the day we will meet our God. Just two weeks ago a preacher was driving home from a Bible class and was killed by a drunk driver. There was no time to say, "Wait a minute, I'm not ready yet." Life and death can be only a split second apart. Greg was granted ten months before his death. I wonder about us.

As I began to get ready to come here today, I thought again

about what Greg would have wanted to do if he were with me visiting a friend's grave. So I scurried through our yard and picked one of each kind of blooming plant, a lilac, narcissus, red tulip, yellow tulip, purple azalea and a bloom from "his" dogwood tree. I know Greg doesn't need this beautiful bouquet here on his grave. He also doesn't need my company; he is not alone. He no longer knows sadness, so doesn't need the tears that dampen the gravestone. Greg now has his heavenly Father who fulfills his every need completely, not in part as I tried to do. He doesn't need the sunshine to break through a cloud; he has the sunlight of God's presence forever. He has no need for my time, for with God time has no beginning or ending — it is eternal. He doesn't even need to know how very much I miss him, think about him, love him and cherish him; he is surrounded by and engulfed in an unbounded sense of security and total serenity. Greg no longer has any needs of any kind; he is at peace with himself, with the world, and with his Creator.

So why am I here? I guess the reason is that once a mother, always a mother. Once a child is born a part of you, it is always a part of you. Once a child is loved, it is always loved. The bond of love is not broken by separation, distance, lack of communication or death. True love that has once found a dwelling place in the heart cannot be tampered with or destroyed. It lives right on into eternity where the Creator of love will show His perfect love.

Will I ever stop missing Greg? Will I ever stop shedding tears or thinking about the many years we had together? I don't think so. The older I get the more I realize how life is so very short. Though Greg no longer needs me, others do and I must daily overcome the struggles within and be aware of my duties. I cannot and do not want to live in the past. This can become a burden to me and those around me. I must strive to live this day as God would have me to live it, not fearing the future, but consistently preparing myself and others for the moment God calls us home to Him.

So many tears have fallen that dampness has helped to clean away the brown winter smudges on the gravestone. The warm sunlight begins to warm my back. I'll be back again to this place where I can be alone with my thoughts and God's comfort as I make an overview of my life and remember all of my responsibilities. Soon I will be with Greg, my mother and my dearest friend whose new grave is just across the path. I need these moments and I thank God for allowing me to come here.

1985

(3 Years)

❖

April 9th, 1985

About ten days less than three years ago, Greg knew his young life was nearing the end, the end of his temporary dwelling place here, and he was preparing to enter the realm God had prepared for him. A year earlier when Greg dedicated his life to his Lord, he still had so much he wanted to do. He wanted to invest his God-given talents into showing love for his fellow man. He didn't want to have to leave so soon.

As I sit here near Greg's gravestone today and see how it has become somewhat weathered from the past three years of rains and temperature changes, I am made aware of how much more beautiful the stone is than when it was first laid. As my finger follows the engravings of Greg's name the paper becomes wet with tears and my heart yields up captured emotions stored there over the last months. Greg bore his name proudly and signed it proudly on his many works of art. Now it is only a still engraving upon a stone on a grassy slope encircled by blooming cherry trees filled with birds singing the song of spring. The comforting, all-powerful presence of our God Almighty surrounds me.

How often I have thought of Mary and Martha and their sorrow over the death of their brother, Lazarus, and then their unsurpassed joy over his resurrection from death only a few days later. Oh, yes, I'd love to have Greg back again for a while, but would I then be willing to let him go a second time? I'm afraid that would be too hard. I'd want to keep him forever. God wants Greg close to Him now and will keep him in His care until we meet again.

When I am out among other people, I constantly see young men that remind me of Greg, or what I think he might look like three years older. This is not something I flood my mind with, it just happens, and suddenly my heart yearns for him. Why do I feel this way?

Reminiscence

Before I left home this morning I picked some lilacs that are not quite open. Greg would laugh at the way they are hanging over the vase and touching the pink ears of the white bunny I placed in the corner of the stone. I miss our secrets, our laughs, our talks and our tears. May God help me daily to better understand His will.

As I leave, I pause at my mother's grave and am reminded of her love, and how God's love and grace allowed her to obey His will in her later years. Across the path at my dear friend's grave, memories of a 43-year friendship cause me to thank God for her love for truth, which led me into His kingdom. They all rest in His peace. Why am I then so sad?

❖

July 29th, 1985

For weeks I knew this day was coming and asked to have it off from work and family responsibilities. Some had forgotten just what the 29th was; time has a way of erasing memories.

Early this morning just a few hours before Sunday turned to Monday in 1963, our little toe-headed Gregory was born, 22 years ago. In 1981 we celebrated his last birthday on our patio, just after he recovered from a near fatal dose of chemotherapy. Weak and hairless, he showed deep appreciation for the love and concern of friends, neighbors and family.

Here at the grave I placed a rose from the bush given in his honor by friends at work. It is fittingly called a peace rose, with soft yellow petals tipped with delicate pink. Greg cherished flowers and tenderly gifted others with them. Along with the cultured rose, I placed a wild pink rose in memory of his mischievous side, but we do all agree that there is no one who can replace the ability Greg had to take almost nothing and create an original gift from it. We allow this special gift to rest with Greg.

As I drove here today I went within a few blocks of a school where Greg's little brother is in a leadership workshop. He has been elected student body president of the junior high for this coming year. He reminds me of Greg, creative, sensitive and organized. A little further down the street I passed the house where I lived with my mom when I got married. That reminded me of my marriage, which later was blessed by the birth of our third son, Gregory. As I turned into another street I saw the fish market where, when I was a child, my mother purchased fish, trying to live economically after our father left us. A little further out of town I passed the funeral home where a service was held for my mother eight years ago. Her grave is here just below Greg's. South on this same street marks the corner where my dearest friend and I met weekly to take violin lessons. Two years ago she was taken away from all of us as a result of cancer. Her stone is just across the path from Greg's.

Why did I choose this street of memories on the way here today? I don't know. I never come this way, but today it just happened. Life contains so much, but in one tiny second it can be gone. God is the Giver and God is the Taker of life and I thank Him that my mother, my friend and my son all rest in peace with Him. The Lord has been gracious to all.

If Greg were with us today I'd probably buy him a new shirt, plaid pants and some nice-smelling after-shave. We would have tried to surprise him with a party; he loved surprises and passed them out generously to others.

Greg also loved challenges and changes. I am reminded of when the chemotherapy destroyed his hair in one day; he shaved his head. He also made it fun by trying on different wigs and enjoyed the comments at school when he went from blond to red. His time was filled with positive ways to cope and live.

Now, time has no meaning with Greg, and birthdays are forever over. He is in eternity where there is no time, no night, and no end to God's love and glory.

There are times when I am alone with my thoughts and everything seems so worthless. Life, love, birth, happiness and material things. They are all so temporary, only here to enjoy for a short period of time, then they are gone or we are taken from them. It is at that moment I ask God to help me understand my purpose in this vast, endless maze of changes.

Am I able and will I be able to daily overcome my feelings and strivings within and lift my eyes continually to God who is the only One who understands and can help? Will I be able to aid others to hold on to the gifts God has given them and encourage those who are in darkness to grasp the light before it is too late?

When my heart is so heavy, I feel I can't fulfill these expectations of God. I am comforted with His promises. He says when we are weak, we are strong. For in turning to Him, though we are weak, He will take our hand and give us the strength to overcome.

Greg would not want me or anyone to lose faith because of him. He wanted to live so as to help others to find eternal life. To lose faith would be to deny God's wisdom in calling Greg home. Why then, am I so sensitive, feeling everything and anything and constantly asking God to help me overcome?

Why can't I just forget the past and go on as though it did not happen. I know some who can do that; I can't.

What I must do is take the past and use it in this present day to the glory of God and His children. If I can't do this, then I need to evaluate my feelings. History of anything or anyone is for us a means whereby we can learn.

I must close now, though I would rather stay here hours upon hours writing and shedding tears, but God didn't call me to continually mourn for the dead in Christ, but to rejoice and tell others of this precious gift of life after death.

As I sit here just a few feet above Greg's stone a young groundskeeper is digging a new grave. On the road above him a hearse drives to another area to lay a body to rest.

If Greg were here today he would say, "It's OK, Mom, don't cry anymore. I'm OK and I want you to be OK." I must go now. I thank God for these moments when I can be alone with my thoughts and memories.

❖

December 18th, 1985

It is cold. I can see my breath in the air, but the sun is trying to warm my quivering body and attempting to dry the tears on my face and the paper as I write. I am all alone at Greg's grave. I had to come; I don't know why. Maybe it is the time of year, the time when everyone thinks of others and what can make them happy.

Greg always wanted everyone to be happy. His little clever gifts and homemade cards with self-created verses were a part of his sharing with others.

This season, for me, has lost something since Greg was called home to his Creator. I can no longer hang the stockings on the fireplace, because Greg had a certain way to hang them that no one else was able to do. They are put away forever. Surprises and excitement of Greg's kind left with him, for they were his specialties.

Quiescent

I miss him so much, still. Will I ever stop missing him? I don't think so. Will I ever stop feeling I want him to be here again?

I know he can't be here; yes, I know this. I am assured he is at peace with everything where he is.

This time of the year the world talks of peace, peace on earth and goodwill to all men. But, real peace, which Greg has become a part of so young in life, is promised by God for those who faithfully follow Him.

As I sit here beside the gravestone, the towering maple tree near me has shed her leaves in various patterns on the graves around. The wind then being her helper has created an accent to Greg's memorial, a large leaf in the right corner and two leaves resting close to each other in the left. I couldn't have done it better myself. I did add a few fir branches and a little holly. Greg doesn't need any decorations or special things to bring joy. He is engulfed in joy, never ending. This gift is more for me, the mother who misses her son so very much. It is like a small token of my love for him.

Greg and I had so many feelings that were entwined and these feelings remain. Though we are separated by death, they cannot be taken away.

Our God and Creator hears my cry, oh so often, as I continue on and reach out to aid others who have lost their children. No, I don't ever want to forget Greg, nor do I want to erase any of my heartfelt feelings. What I do want to do is to help others, if God permits.

We are so blessed that Greg was ready to meet his God; that is a comfort immeasurable. How would I cope if he had not been? I don't know, and I pray I will never lose a child who is not secure in God's hands. May God ever help me to teach and train so others may receive the same blessings as Greg.

I must go; school bus driving calls me away from this serene place where I desire to stay for many more hours. I pray God will help me overcome, lift my tear-streaked face and allow these moments of closeness with Him to fill my needs so I can share with others.

The sun passes behind a big fir tree. The air and ground are cold. I must go.

1986

(4 Years)

February 6th, 1986

The gravestone is cold and damp; the grass is wet with dew drops of fog. Fog hovers over the entire vast sea of graves, some highlighted by flowers, others unnoticed in the grass.

It hasn't been that long since Greg's lifeless body was lowered here to rest. Today as I sit here shivering, the wind whipping the pages as I write, my tears flow slowly down my cold cheeks. Inside, my heart weeps silently knowing God is also here to share in my sadness.

Why do I keep coming here when it makes my whole body ache? Why do I even want to feel this way? Why can't I just live with the memories of Greg that surround me daily and not remind myself of his death? If I knew the answers I wouldn't be here. I wouldn't allow the damp fog to nip my nose and invade my body causing it to quiver.

Is it because here I can write and can go into my innermost feelings? Is it because here I can grieve in the presence of the One who called Greg to join Him? Is it here I can ask all the questions I keep secluded, knowing God Almighty comforts me and allows me to pour out these cries?

I have placed some pink primroses on the grave. They will stay here for a few days, then wither, as all of God's creation must do. God gives life, and God takes life.

My fingers are becoming too cold to write; my body yearns for a warm place. I must go for now.

❖

April 21ˢᵗ, 1986

Today four years ago I spoke my last words to Greg, "I love you so much," then I gave him my last hug and kiss. About one hour later he took his last breath and passed into God's hands forever.

Those last minutes are as though on a tape that has instant recall on days like today, but also at other times when I stop in the hall to dust his pictures, hug his friends, or pick up something he himself wrote, made or painted.

Here in the cemetery there is not a cloud in the warm, blue sky. The sun warms the back of my pink sweater. Again I picked some garden flowers, lilacs, azaleas, rhododendrons, dogwood blossoms from "his" tree, and of course a pink carnation. They all give a special touch to the stone. I miss Greg so very much.

Why do I always wish Greg was here when he can be where there are no tears that now blur my vision and drip from my cheeks, where he won't have to experience the death of his loved ones or friends, and where he now rests in eternal peace?

Greg and I had a bond that I think each parent has with each child in a different way. We enjoyed the same things — music, surprise parties, unexpected little notes and cards. We loved the beauty of the seasons, the flowers, trees, and water. We liked to redecorate rooms, arrange bouquets, hang streamers or a poster for a special day for someone. Greg burned many midnight hours doing just such things, things for the happiness of others. I miss him daily.

If Greg had lost one of his brothers, sisters or friends, he would not want to forget the feelings, the love and the closeness they shared. He would be writing poems, songs, painting pictures about the one gone on before him. How do I know that? I just do! He would be with me here today.

Almost ten years ago we buried my mother just a few feet below

Greg's grave. God did not reveal to me then that my son's grave would be near hers, nor did He choose to tell me that a year after my son's death I would lose my long time school friend and her grave would be across from the other two.

Up until Greg's death I thought my faith in God was firm, sure and steadfast, able to withstand the strongest shakes. God's plan was different from my plan, for I had not planned on such early deaths in our family. My plan was to raise my children in the Lord, see them marry Christians, enjoy all the grandchildren and then when I was old and they were all stable, God could let me pass on, knowing all would be well.

Because I didn't understand when God said, "My ways are not your ways," my faith was put to a test. I must constantly face reality as an individual in the presence of God, alone. This faith cannot be dependent on my husband, children, friends or fellow Christians. It must be a faith, regardless of circumstances, that will carry me right through to the end, where I will then meet my friend, my mother and my son again.

This is a daily struggle for me, as it should have been all along. I guess I just thought I had it made. Possibly I would have even sat down on a park bench and rested when I should have been proving my faith. God knew what was best for me, He loves me more than I can even understand, just as He loves Greg, my mother and my friend.

I must go now and drive the bus. Life goes on. It is meant to, until God sees it is time to call me home. I want to be ready. I pray for daily strength to overcome. Greg would want each of us to carry on so we can all be together once again.

July 29ᵗʰ, 1986

Twenty-three years ago Gregory Dean Earnhart was born.

If Greg were here he'd say "thank you" for the rose I brought and thank me for the visit. He wouldn't want me to say "good-bye" for he didn't like tears or parting. He always wanted everyone to be happy.

Today I can see him as a 23-year-old— mature, handsome and interested in the welfare of others, but I must accept the fact that he is no longer with us here and nevermore will be. I must realize I will never hear his voice on the phone saying, "Hi, Mom," nor will he pop in about dinner time and lift the lids on the pots on the stove and say, "Sure smells good, Mom." There will be no more sweet notes, poems, letters or surprise packages designed especially for me from him, nor will I hear his footsteps crossing the floor above me in that special quick gait of his. I will never hear him sing in another musical, or observe him in another play. His midnight oil will nevermore burn as he sketches, draws and designs posters, logos and pictures. I can't buy him any more of his favorite shirts or socks, nor can I press his clothes before a performance.

I also can't look into his deep blue eyes and read the messages of his heart, or listen to his problems, his funny stories or daily happenings. I won't be able to wash his clothes, buy him ice cream or feel his skin and know he is here.

What I can do is cry, as I now am doing. I can also miss him as I also now do and wait for the day I can see him, as I now wait.

Why don't I just forget all the years, the days, the minutes, the seconds we were together? Because I don't want to.

Why don't I just close the chapter, put the book away and say it is all over? Because I don't want to.

Greg is my son, so how can I say he was my son? It is true he is God's son, so in a sense he now belongs to God. I do like to say, "Yes, we have a son who is now with his Creator. His spirit didn't die, it lives on."

Sometimes my heart yearns so deeply for Greg that I can hardly understand or overcome the feelings inside. Sometimes I want him here, I want to go to him, I want to talk to him, I want to see him, I want to touch him, I want to hear him say, "It's OK, Mom, don't worry about me."

I know he is all right. I know he is happy, content, safe, cared for and at peace with himself and God, but moms always need assurance that their children are all right. Yes, God does give me this assurance. I just need to seek it and ask for it.

Just before I came here I had lunch with Greg's younger brother who is a waiter in a very lovely restaurant. How thankful I am to have him; he helps to fill the void left by Greg. He has talents in many of the same areas as his brother; they encouraged each other in using them. Greg's little brother also has ways that remind me of him. His older brother helped form Greg's creative spirit and his older sister instilled within him order and loyalty. So, Greg lives on among us and I thank God for him, the other children, and his father, who daily give me a little bit of Greg's spirit.

It is quiet now, everyone has gone. A cool breeze touches my tears and almost chills me. I must go now. It's time to see about my family, cook dinner for them and continue my duties on this earth as God has instructed. Help me, dear God, to never stray from the goals ahead. Help me to encourage the other children so they, too, will be able to one day be at home with You.

❖

December 23rd, 1986

The sun came out, as if someone knew,
    I wanted to spend some time here with you.

Of course you are gone, where I am not,
    But my heart, my all, embraces you in thought.

I want to hug you, whisper in your ear,
    Tell you of my love and wishes for the coming year.

I miss you at the table as we all bow to pray,
    Hand in hand together in a very special way.

I miss your cheerfulness at special times like these,
    Always caring, always giving, always wanting to please.

Nature beat me to the grave and left her sign of care,
    Two leaves clasped together help today my grief to bear.

I always come here alone, even you can't come with me,
    Nor can I come with you, we are separated you see.

But Greg, it won't be forever, God says we'll meet again,
    Our meeting will be wonderful, we don't know just when.

So, sweetheart, I must go, to my pilgrim walk here below,
    The wind is cold, the grass is wet, my writing becomes slow.

I will come again to be with you in thought and prayer,
    I know God holds you close and His glory you do share.

A part of me is now with our God and Greg that is you,
    So help me dear God not to fall, that I might be there too.

1987

(5 Years)

January 29th, 1987

Dear God, please understand why I come here all the time and say the same things over and over again.

I know Greg doesn't need me; I know he is at peace; I know he is happy and surrounded by love.

But, as a mother, I want to ask Thee to keep him close, just for me, because I cannot hug him anymore.

I know also that he doesn't need a hug; I know that and I thank Thee that I can come here to write and feel Thy closeness, our great Creator, God, gracious Savior and Guide.

I could never go on without Thee. Help me always to overcome. Thank you.

❖

April 21ˢᵗ, 1987

Another year now has gone by,
  That makes five and still I cry.

I cry for his face, I cry for his smile,
  My heart yearns to see him, it will be a while.

Will I ever forget this day in Greg's life,
  The day he left for a life free of strife?

I would that I could rejoice more in this day,
  The day Greg knew was his, but feared in a way.

The day in his youth he could not fully know,
  The day his mother didn't want to come, even though.

We all knew God would soon guide him home to live;
  I hoped, I was selfish, I didn't really want to give.

Looking back I can see it was God's will I tried to deny;
  I didn't want to believe in separation, that Greg would die.

I so wanted him to live, to be with me, to be well,
  Now I know God knew my thoughts; He tried to tell.

He tried to tell me Greg needed to go home, to be free,
  It takes a lot sometimes for a mother to really want to see.

Each child born is a blessing only mothers can feel,
  The bond is so strong, it is forever, it is real.

Death cannot break this bond, nor will it even strain;
  It grows stronger, it is there until the two meet again.

But while I sit here at the grave and wait out this time,
    I must keep busy in God's kingdom, then joy will be mine.

When someday Greg and I once again walk hand in hand,
    It won't be a short walk, but forever with God so grand.

Now God, grant me mercy, patience, love and hope,
    That I will always trust in Thee, please help me cope.

A part of your creation, a leaf from a majestic tree,
    Once again has fallen on Greg's name, to touch it for me.

Thank you for these moments, in my heart I sigh,
    You understand, You give me comfort when I cry.

You know I'll be back, if You allow me to come later,
    Here alone with memories of Greg, and You, God,
        his Maker.

July 29th, 1987

Twenty-four years ago today Greg entered this world in peace, no cares, no concerns, no sorrows. Five years ago he was granted these same blessings, only for eternity in the arms of God. So, when I left the house today to come here to the grave, I picked a peace rose from "Greg's" rose bush to place by his name. The peace Greg had within at birth he now has in its fullest meaning forever and ever.

Peaceful

Just yesterday a young man was buried. He too had struggled with cancer for many years. I understood him and I could feel with his mother; we all cried together. He is now in the hands of his Maker.

Peace, what is it?

As I sit here at my son's grave on his 24th birthday, the grave that was freshly dug a little more than five years ago for his cancer-ridden body, I contemplate what true peace really is.

We talk about a peacefully sleeping baby, a peaceful setting, peaceful atmosphere, or a peaceful feeling, all allowing us to feel warm, secure and content inside. Such peaceful times however, can change quickly in only a few seconds to an almost hostile setting. A sudden noise can rouse a peaceful baby, sudden storms can disturb a peaceful atmosphere, or "This is the emergency room; your son has been in an accident," can upset a peaceful feeling.

At funerals these words are very often spoken, "May the soul rest in peace." Is peace just a quietness that overcomes the being, an undisturbed existence, a feeling of freedom from pain and sorrow?

True peace is given only by One, God Almighty, for those who fight the good fight of faith as the apostle Paul was able to do. It is a peace that surpasses all understanding. It is in God's realm; it is eternal, reserved for His children.

As I again look closer at the rose here on Greg's grave, the peace rose, I ask myself why it was given this name. Is it because of its delicate yellow petals, so elegantly outlined in warm pink colors that soothe, colors that give warmth? It has an unsurpassed beauty, a beauty only our loving Creator could have designed; it offers up a feeling of peace.

Greg was one who always sought after peace in the way he understood it. He settled fights and quarrels. He sat hours at his desk creating cards, verses, posters or drawings that would bring about joy to others, something to promote peace. Greg was not aware at the time that all his efforts to bring peace and happiness would one day, in his young life, lead him into a peace that was everlasting, a peace he had not yet even sought, a restful peace with his Creator, a peace only God has the authority to grant, a peace He grants to those who seek it through Him.

God's peace is dependent on nothing and no one, for He Himself is peace. Everlasting peace is a gift in death. We often cry for peace in the world, but it takes only one bomb threat, a single terrorist, or an all-out war to turn peace into disaster. The peace of God cannot be taken away from a child of God, or disturbed or destroyed. God created peace, and He is the ruler and the distributor of peace.

It is this peace that now surrounds Greg and it is this peace that today comforts me. As I look into the deep blue sky and observe the white cloud formations, view the acres of fresh green lawns surrounded by plush trees, smell the sweetness of blooming bushes and feel the sun's warmth on the gravestone that bears the name "Gregory Dean Earnhart," then I know God is alive, He is here and He is my peace.

❖

December 22nd, 1987

The grass is wet, rain drops glisten on each blade;
> It's cold, the sun casts a shadow over Greg's grave.

I had to come to think of Greg on the day he loved so much;
> He'd hide his gifts from us and give them one final touch.

Greg's greatest joy was to make others smile, to give;
> It is his spirit that lingers with us, it continues to live.

As a little fellow he'd wrap an old book, drawing or toy;
> Everyone who came his way, left with a token of his joy.

This year we all give thanks around the table hand in hand,
> But, two hands have already gone on to the promised land.

Our whole family will be gathered, everyone will be home;
> Even Greg is home, home with God, never more to be alone.

1988

(6 Years)

April 20th, 1988

Six years ago on Wednesday night April 21st, 1982, I was alone in the room with Greg. We took turns staying home with him day and night because he was so very ill. His older brother was to take the next shift.

Greg was very weak, but he talked some and I made the necessary preparations for his bedtime. It was a special time for the two of us, but that Wednesday night Greg was exceptionally tired. He wanted to rest. His breathing was burdened and my heart ached for him as I watched him take each breath. I read him the 23rd Psalm and gave him hugs and kisses. I wanted to hold him longer, but he couldn't breathe too well when I pulled him close to me, so I had to give him breathing room. We said goodnight to each other, and I took my place on the floor near his bed. I was recording the day's medical happenings when he moved his leg to another position. The pain must have been almost unbearable for him. He then became very quiet and I thought he had gone to sleep.

The rest of the family returned in a few minutes and checked on us; all seemed to be peaceful, but somehow there was a feeling of fear in my heart. I couldn't keep my eyes off Greg. He was so very still. His dad and I tried to arouse him, but we couldn't. The evening before Greg had dropped into a short coma, but was revived by extra oxygen. This time nothing caused him to respond. We called the local oxygen specialists; they came right over. Our other children came and filled the room. Greg's head was on my lap, others held him tight and he took his last breaths.

Tonight as I recall these moments I can hardly bear the sorrow inside of me, nor control the tears as they flow down my face.

I miss Greg.

I didn't want to lose him. I wanted him to live and enjoy life and allow God to work in this life. Now, as then, it doesn't matter what I want, but what God felt was best for Greg and for all of us who still struggle with the burdens of our own lives.

Greg's struggle ended six years ago, but in my heart Greg is still with me. He will always be. Thank you, God.

The 23rd Psalm

The Lord is my shepherd,
    I shall not want.
He makes me lie down
    in green pastures;
He leads me beside quiet waters.
    He restores my soul;
He guides me in the paths of righteousness
    for His name's sake.
Even though I walk through
    the valley of the shadow of death,
I fear no evil;
    for Thou art with me;
Thy rod and Thy staff,
    they comfort me.
Thou doest prepare a table
    before me in the presence of my enemies;
Thou hast anointed my head with oil,
    My cup overflows.
Surely goodness and lovingkindness
    will follow me all the days of my life,
And I will dwell in the house
    of the Lord forever.

July 26th, 1988

The sun is going down here at the cemetery. The day has been hot, but now a warm breeze whispers through the trees and it seems so very peaceful. In three days Greg would have been 25. We won't be here, we'll be on our way to Kentucky to see the other Earnharts, others Greg's age, others who have finished college and can now go out in life. Greg never had that opportunity and it will be hard for me to see others who have. No, I won't be mad or angry, or jealous, or unhappy with those whom God has allowed to live and enjoy life here, but deep in my heart I will miss Greg's warm spirit among them. He loved being with family and feeling a part of the family's love.

I think of him when I see some handsome blond fellow with blue eyes, about Greg's age and size. I miss him, I miss watching him grow into manhood, and I miss his positive and happy spirit.

I know though that for him to live would not have been what God intended and God always knows what is best for each of us.

Inside of Greg's vibrant personality was a deep sensitivity for others and also for himself. He suffered terribly when doing wrong. He hurt when seeing someone else suffer. There were events in his life from time to time that made it hard to cope — temptations pushed on the door as they do in the lives of all our children. He had placed his life in his Savior's hands; he could tap into God's help and strength for the road ahead.

God was merciful to Greg, calling him home, allowing him to find everlasting peace, free from pain, hurt and temptations.

In the final words, minutes before his parting, I said, "Greg, God has been so good to you." Greg answered, "I know, Mom."

Greg knew then, and I know now, that it was out of God's deepest love and mercy that Greg was allowed to go home. Yes, I know and I believe, but it doesn't always erase my feelings, the feelings I have when I see others and wish he were here.

I ask God to forgive me for these conflicting feelings; they erupt when I least expect and they overcome my whole being.

Why am I driven to come here again and again? I do not know; the desire is so strong. Here I can be alone with my thoughts and prayers.

I pray Thee, oh God, allow me to grieve, mourn and weep,
　　　　but don't allow me to give up hope.
Give me the strength to work through each weak moment,
　　　　give me assurance that in Thee I can cope.
Guide me then to help others,
　　　　to show them Your peace,
　　　　Your mercy and Your love.
Help us together to understand the reasons,
　　　　to see it as preparation for our home above.
Let me rejoice through the river of tears,
　　　　lift my face,
　　　　help me feel Thy presence, know Thy promises,
　　　　help me smile.
Allow me the same mercy and grace you granted Greg
　　　　that I might be with Him, with Thee,
　　　　in the great after-a-while.

❖

December 22ⁿᵈ, 1988

It's cold and gray here at the grave,
    the sky turns dusk above;
  But my heart swells and my eyes fill
    with an ever present love.

A love for someone I miss,
    someone I wish were here but has been called home;
  Oh, yes, I know he is safe; he is well
    and in God's care he will never be alone.

I am the one who sits here alone;
    others don't understand why I'm here in the cold;
  Maybe it is because I can't seem to give up dreams;
    it will all pass, I have been told.

I don't wish to bring Greg back to life,
    to pain and troubles, to me;
  But I do wish to remember all in my heart
    until we meet in eternity.

Darkness creeps over me, I shiver;
    I must go back to my home now;
  Greg would understand why I came;
    we felt each other's needs, somehow.

So, God, I ask Thee for patience, don't leave;
    I beg of Thee to remain;
  Someday I pray I will overcome,
    or will it not be until I meet Greg again?

1989

(7 Years)

April 20ᵗʰ, 1989

It's cold, rainy and damp; the gravestones are covered with wet grass. The clouds hang heavy as does my heart. Tears and rain moisten my face and clothes. I can't stay long, but I had to come.

Seven years ago Greg knew his hours were numbered. He knew his life on earth was fading, yet he never grew bitter or angry; he tried to cheer others.

He knew he had to cross over Jordan alone, alone as he often was with his thoughts and unexpressed fears, alone to answer to God for his life here, alone without Mom and Dad to help lift him over the last crevice. Greg had said his final words, knowing God had been gracious to him.

As I sit here I beg God to be gracious with me, with my fears, my many weaknesses and at times the still gnawing guilt for Greg's early death. Why didn't I realize he was ill? Why didn't I spend more time with him?

God knows my heart and knows how much I want to write about Greg. Some day, if He wills, I will be allowed this task.

Seven years seem like seven days, like a week ago when we were here at this place, Greg's burial site. It is still so vivid and the same feelings burn within me. Will I ever forget? No I can't. I don't want to and with God's help I'll always remember what Greg means to me and to those whose lives he touched.

❖

The rain it pours, I'm wet and cold,
    I must go back.
  Why did I come to place flowers, to write, to weep?
    God knows, sometimes I don't; I lose track.

Seven years is like a week,
    a week a year, a year a span.
  Time has no meaning,
    death surely comes to every man.

It was just yesterday
    we laid Greg in peace to rest.
  He had suffered, he'd overcome,
    he'd passed the test.

I pray I can do as well, be strong,
    not falter or fall.
  Greg helps me take courage,
    keep going, give God my all.

Thank you, God, for Greg's short life,
    his example to me.
  Though I am undeserving, walk with me,
    until Greg I may see.

❖

August 2nd, 1989

Inside, within, there is a pull toward times
     when memories especially
  Live,

To come to Greg's grave, alone, to write, to pray,
    To give.

To share my feelings, my thoughts, to spill my secret
    Grief,

Only God knows the depth from which I desire to seek
    Relief.

Not relief from the love that still yearns strong
    Within,

Nor from the desire to come here where I have so often
    Been.

But to share my hidden grief
     with Someone Who knows, Who
  Cares,

I feel my burdens lifted, my spirit soothed, in His love He
    Bears.

In a sense this is a place where God and I
    Meet,

I know I must come, to pray, to sit at His
    Feet,

To gain new strengths, to go forward in my
    Life,

Seek comfort, learn mercy, understand my role as His child,
      a mother, a
    Wife.

He has never forsaken me, His presence is, oh, so very
    Real,

When words come hard and tears flow, He knows how I
    Feel.

I come here for myself, though selfish it may sometimes
    Seem,

Greg's needs are fulfilled, God's promises are not just a
    Dream.

I seek a closeness to Greg in a way I cannot even
    Explain,

And here on his grave I find it, in spite of the grief and
    Pain.

Greg needed to go home, home to a place where he could
    Rest,

He had battled hard in his short life, for Greg, God knew
    Best.

1990

(8 Years)

❖

April 21ˢᵗ, 1990

Eight years to the day
      they carried our Greg away.

"Hold him tight," I had said as he breathed his last,
      "keep him close and warm."
One by one the family enclosed around him
      as if to shelter him from harm.

We were a fortress, a whole,
      one heart and one soul.

We witnessed death as a terrible, devastating, separating pain.
      "Now we know why we are Christians," I said,
      "we will see Greg again."

Thank God for promises, for hope,
      for mercy to help cope.

Each day I pray for strength, courage, faithfulness,
      and for God's boundless love;
These blessings guided Greg to that moment
      when God reached down to him from above.

So why am I at the grave, here?
      Why is this place so dear?

You'd think I'd forget, I'd quit coming to write and pray;
      I'd close the chapter and move on,
But I'm not ready to finalize, to end; I want to keep
      Greg's memories alive like a beautiful song.

In Greg's siblings I can see,
    some of him in them, just for me.

In a way he lives on, not in body, but in little ways,
    in feelings, in love, in spirit, in his place at home.
  I thank God for reminders, that I not forget,
    for we will be together again around God's throne.

❖

April 21ˢᵗ, 1990
at Greg's grave for Mike

Other reminders linger, like my friend Mike,
    a young man with cancer we've talked about before;
  He has reminded me of my son Greg
    from the day we met on my school bus,
    sharing cookies and so much more.

Mike and I have spent hours through the years talking,
    sharing and just having a lot of fun;
  I guess he needed me and I needed him,
    though I was not aware he even knew about my son.

Now his battle too is almost over,
    I can see him slowly growing weary and I know;
  His hour will soon come; his body is thin,
    his once quick wit is now a little slow.

Just last night I was called; I went to his home
    and sat in a chair near to his bed;
  Though unable to speak many words,
    he wanted to be a part of everything that was said.

He held firmly to my hand
>   while his brother rubbed away pain,
>   oxygen helped each breath of life;
> Mike still has so much to offer each of us,
>   bravery, courage and love, even in great strife.

Like my son, he is always "fine";
>   no soldier has fought a more valiant, confident,
>   fearless fight;
> I had to leave, I wanted to stay;
>   I kissed quickly his forehead, "I love you," I said,
>   "I love you too," he whispered.

Good night, Mike, good night.

1991

(9 Years)

April 24ᵗʰ, 1991

Nine years ago today I was here,
    as were others too;
  It was yesterday, it seems to me,
    though maybe not for you.

Now for me the cool wind has pushed
    the rain and dark clouds away;
  A few rays of sun begin to warm
    the gravestone on this typical April day.

We laid Greg's body to rest where today
    hills of graves lie one against another;
  My longtime school friend, her father,
    and just below my own dear mother.

All have passed on, their walks finished,
    each according to God's gracious will;
  Now we who remain must wait, God will call,
    may He help us be faithful still.

Together forever, no more good-byes, no tears,
    how glorious that will be;
  Help me, oh God, to keep going, my head up,
    so as Thy pathway to clearly see.

I know Greg suffered in silence,
    he didn't want to burden us most of the time;
  But as a mother, I could sense,
    I could feel the pain and fear as if it were mine.

Before any of us knew,
> Greg felt his days were numbered, they were few;
>> He was ready to go home; he trusted God,
>>> he had faith he would live anew.

Greg's soul is secure in God's love,
> no evil tempter knocking at his door;
>> Please God, watch over the other children,
>>> prepare them for what is in store.

Help each one, daily, see the straight way
> to the heavenly goal;
>> That someday, we will all be together again,
>>> each and every soul.

Now, God I thank you for comfort as I weep,
> but I am made to be glad;
>> for Your grace, Your mercy, Your salvation,
>>> and all the blessings we've had.

Please go with me now, take my hand,
> help me pass each and every test;
>> So I may be allowed to be at peace with Greg,
>>> when I am finally laid to rest.

Comforting

❖

July 29ᵗʰ, 1991

The bees sip the honey from the
    clover surrounding Greg's grave;
    They have come here the past nine years
      to sip and to save.

God created them as he did our son,
    with a purpose, a goal;
    But God gave Greg something special,
      a living soul.

A small squirrel from the woods creeps toward me,
    not shy;
    Near the grave he staggers, gasps for air,
      lies down to die.

None of God's creation can know
    the length of their duty here;
    God alone keeps the list, for us a mystery,
      for Him it is clear.

Not even a small sparrow is unaccounted for,
    God knows each one;
    His love is endless, for you, for me,
      and for my son.

No, I don't always understand every feeling,
    renewed eruptions of pain;
    God promises me comfort though,
      knowing I will see Greg again.

It is with this hope of spending eternity
      with those who have gone on before,
   That I greet each day knowing God
      has something better for me in store.
So on this earth I must stay, at least for today,
      or for the time God gives;
   Then with my son, I will go to the One
      whose promise forever lives.

Help me, God, to keep the faith,
      stay strong during the length of my stay;
   Knowing as Greg was called, so must I,
      prepare me for that day.

1992

(10 Years)

April 21ˢᵗ, 1992

The storm has passed, it is cool,
 I linger, all is wet.

All day it has stormed a little,
  then sun, clouds or rain;
 But now it is still and cold,
  the sky prepares to hide again.

Scattered graves are marked with flowers
  from the holiday last week;
 Today I am alone,
  for most there is here nothing to seek.

I don't come here to find someone or something
  others might see;
 Solace, God's presence,
  comfort and peace is what I seek; it is free.

True, God is no nearer to me here
  than many other places I've been;
 It's where I can lose my thoughts
  in God's great promises to men.

As clouds take on new shapes
  and change from dark gray to white;
 I can know God lives, is in control,
  has all things in His loving might.

Trees continue to bloom year after year,
    others are green and tall;
  This world God has created is perfect,
    it is His; to be enjoyed by all.

Greg was once a part of this miracle,
    this splendor, this gift of love;
  Greg's paintings, his speech, his life,
    all expressed an awe for God above.

Now Greg is a part of another world,
    a place of rest, an eternal home;
  The beauty he once painted with a brush,
    is now a reality all his own.

How can I thank God for His kindness,
    His grace, for hearing my prayers;
  I know He is good, He is kind,
    He is gracious and for His own He cares.

My plea to God is for more than wealth, or fame
    or to even take first place;
  It is for my children to be prepared
    for the day they meet God face to face.

Greg has gone to meet his Maker.
    God called him; He made the choice.
  Yes, it has been hard;
    but each one of us will also heed to His voice.

It will be then, we must give an answer,
    time to change will be no more;
  As Greg, we must be ready,
    so we can meet our Savior on the other shore.

May God help me to grow each day,
   no matter how difficult it might be;
  Show me my duties, aid me in completing them
   and always abide with me.

May Greg's brothers and sisters, their children,
   though still so small;
  Prepare themselves to meet our God,
   so He can lift them up when they fall.

There is no other way to be happy,
   to be sure of the destiny of our soul,
  Than to serve Him forever;
   help us all, dear God, to stay in this role.

Today as I sit here, listen to the birds
   and ponder the ten years just past,
  I'm reminded how quickly years vanish;
   our turn to meet God is approaching fast.

The sun greets me through the clouds,
   I am cold, I must go for today;
  With deep gratitude I leave;
   my walk with God continues, with Him I will stay.

Maybe God has something else for me to do,
   soon or in the coming years;
  I want to prepare myself, serve Him,
   be able to meet Him with joy, not fears.

I thank God for the many lessons I've learned
   through Greg's death, the pain and grief;
  May God be given the glory.
   May He ever guide us and strengthen our belief.

❖

July 29ᵗʰ, 1992

I brought a little red flower
    with a shiny yellow face
    and laid it at the top of Greg's gravestone.
  It makes me think of Greg
    who 28 years ago entered this world like a flower,
    only to leave it later, alone.

Alone in the sense I couldn't go with him,
    only hold him tight as his spirit parted
    and they took him away.
  Did Greg feel alone, did he know we were there?
    Did he understand our good-byes
    were until another day?

I feel assured he heard us
    and could feel us holding him close.
    He knew God's presence, His mercy,
    His grace and might.
  Greg was not alone, not then or now.
    As we let go of Greg's hand
    God took it and led him on through the night.

Today there will be no birthday party for Greg,
    just warm, fond memories of the eighteen
    we all celebrated with him.
  Birthdays belonged to Greg, he made surprises for all.,
    So today we rejoice even though
    his day will never come again.

The spot Greg had in our family can never be filled,
    it is empty but full, full of memories,

memories that will never fade.
We speak of him, tell on him, laugh about him
and remember his face even as I sit here
where his body once was laid.

Sometimes I think of a handsome, blond,
blue-eyed young man,
like maybe our Greg would one day have become;
Yet at the same time I thank God he was spared
additional grief and sorrow
and was allowed to go home.

God has been so good to us,
we enjoy so many blessings,
His love is truly divine.
May I be ready, too, when he calls;
may I, as Greg,
feel His hand reach down and take mine.

Finality

1993

(11 Years)

❖

April 21ˢᵗ, 1992

It's windy, it's sunny,
   it's cloudy and now it's cool.
  It sprinkles, it clears, blue sky appears;
    there is no rule.

So it was with Greg, his life, his death,
   from beginning to end.
  He laughed, he loved, he wept,
    like the elements there was no pretend.

When storms came, he put down an anchor,
   he weathered, he overcame.
  For Greg there was never a doubt
    that a rainbow always came after the rain.

He was intensely involved in life, in its vast beauty;
   it was for him to live.
  In each day he found happiness
    in his ever-fervent desire to give.

He was able to put himself in others' shoes, bear their
   hearts, himself he forgot.
  It was not a heavy burden he had to bear, it was light;
    he chose his own lot.

The world gave Greg excitement,
   this was obvious to all those he had around,
  But inside he had a special Guide, he was on his way;
    he was homeward bound.

Here nothing remains now but his gravestone
  discolored by the years.
  I can't hold Greg close; I can't even explain
   why there are still tears.

But Greg would understand if he were here with me
  at the grave of another;
  "You'll see him again, he is with God,
   he is much better off, it's OK, Mother."

God knew the path Greg needed to walk;
  together the two of them never broke step.
  Yes, Greg stumbled, he wavered, he fell,
   God helped him up; the goal was already set.

Death has no rules,
  actually there is no game we can play;
  God has the directions, He knows our time,
   help us, God, we pray.

There was sun, there was wind,
  there were clouds and it was cool;
  It sprinkled, it cleared, blue sky appeared,
   surely there was no rule.

❖

July 29ᵗʰ, 1993

What would he look like,
    how would he be?
    Would he still have a bucket of dreams
     with a spirit so free?

Maybe he'd have a family
    of four or six,
Teaching his children
    to paint or carve on a stick.

Probably his blond hair would be darker,
    or even balding on top;
I think he would be slender,
    in spite of eating a lot.

His smile would be the same,
    like his hugs and his voice;
Fulfilling the needs of others,
    would still be his first choice.

Why do I sit here and ponder
    just how Greg would be today?
I'm not really sure,
    but somehow it helps to take the hurt away.

Possibly it makes me feel like a part of him
    remains here with me;
Just like a part of me went with him,
    this feeling will always be.

This part cannot be replaced by anyone,
  only a mother knows;
 Though not in body, but in spirit,
  where the child is, the mother goes.

No, I don't want it to seem like I doubt God's choice,
  His calling Greg home;
 God's grace overwhelms me, this day,
  too masterful for this meager poem.

Neither do I wish for Greg to be here with me,
  suffering, weak and ill;
 The choice was not mine, nor is it today;
  it was God's choice, His will.

Greg will never be tempted again,
  his fight is forever finished, he rests;
 God designed His will so those who keep the faith
  will pass all the tests.

So, daily I struggle with weaknesses, inadequacies,
  with rocks in my path,
 And thank the One who crossed Greg over,
  He will guide me also with His staff.

What more can a mother pray for,
  in what else can she place her hope;
 She rejoices knowing her child's soul is secure,
  God's promises help her cope.

As I leave the grave today,
  I know in Whom I have believed,
  in Whom I place my trust;
 I hope to return, if God wills,
  to this place to write and pray,
  it seems I must.

1994

(12 Years)

April 21ˢᵗ, 1994

"Help Me to Walk in Your Shoes"

I understand,
      I know just how you must feel;

It took my son Greg's death
      to make it all real.

For years I thought I understood,
      I thought I knew;

Like the day I came with open arms
      to comfort you.

I tried within to imagine
      just how it would be,

If a child of mine were to be taken
      away from me.

Deeply I searched for words,
      the right things to say,

I felt, just maybe,
      I might take some of the pain away.

But your eyes revealed something
      I didn't quite understand;

Your body seemed weary
      as I reached for your hand.

It was a language so foreign;
  I felt somewhat lost;

I want to learn, what will it take;
  what is the cost?

You needed someone who understood,
  had been there like you.

I looked around, I was made aware,
  true comforters were few.

That night I prayed for wisdom,
  to show me a way in due time;

To be able to slip into your shoes
  and make your feelings mine.

The time then came too quickly,
  the course was offered and yet,

The curriculum was overwhelming;
  would I willingly accept?

As I sit at Greg's grave, alone,
  on this beautiful spring day;

I am assured God's plan was fulfilled
  so I can truly say:

I understand,
  I know now just how you must feel;

It took my son Greg's death
  to make it all real.

May I use every crossing of a bridge,
  each scaling of a wall and every finishing of a race,

help me put one of my feet, if not two,
  in your shoes and let God set our pace.

❖

July 29ᵗʰ, 1994

A new grave of my dear friend's mother,
       beside her father, near hers,
       across the way;
    Tells me life is fleeting, it is unsure;
       God did not bring us all
       to this earth to stay.

On this side of the path is the grave of my own Mother
       and of Greg,
       our dear son;
    Today is his 31st birthday,
       he'd be a man
       were it not that his walk is already done.

He finished before he had really begun
       to take stride,
       to seek and to find;
    Like all young men he dreamed of college, a job,
       a family
       and peace of mind.

Greg didn't have to choose,
       he never had to leave home,
       it was easier that way;
    From his deathbed in his own room
       he was transferred
       to God's home to stay.

The last few weeks have been filled
       with reminders of cancer, AIDS,
       miscarriages, accidents and more;

Not a one of us can know
   just what our friends, loved ones
   or even ourselves have in store.

We run, we comfort, we cry,
      we write, we cook,
      we pray and we call,
   Yes, God's children do suffer and even die,
      but for us it is an open door,
      not a wall.

God waits at the door,
      He watches,
      He knows just when we will be coming through.
   Everything is ready,
      His promise is real,
      now the rest is left up to me and to you.

Greg was allowed to enter and he is safe,
      though the last few steps were difficult
      and he feared;
   In his final minutes we read from God's word,
      he was then able to make ready, to let go
      as death neared.

This day I am deeply moved and ever thankful,
      I wish to thank our God
      from the depth of my aching heart.
   He is the One who gives me hope,
      provides courage each day
      so I can begin with a fresh start.

Why has God allowed me to live,
      to be here,
      to still walk On this earth?
   This must be His plan for me,
      for I know He has been my Guide
      since the day of birth.

Looking around me at the graves of my friend's parents,
  my mother,
   Greg and my dear friend,
 I can think back how God's will
   had a purpose in all their lives
   up to the very end.

As a young girl my friend and her mother
   led me to the truth,
   I was taught and obeyed.
 Later my sister, my mother,
   then our family followed God's calling
   as did our son Greg.

So let us never doubt the power
   of one seed of truth,
   it can accomplish so very much.
 May God be praised for all these blessings,
   for every heart God's mercy
   was allowed to touch.

I thank God for these minutes,
   for these opportunities to express my feelings,
   to pray;
 I don't know how long I will be allowed to come here,
   but I thank our Creator
   especially for this day.

I must be on my way,
   it is clouding over,
   it could rain in a little while.
 Help me, oh God, to honor Thee,
   be a willing worker,
   and do it all with a smile.

1995

(13 Years)

April 21ˢᵗ, 1995

It swells inside, I cannot hide
    The tears, I cry, but why?
  He had to leave, this I believe, though
    It was hard to say good-bye.

I never see anyone, but me alone,
    Sitting, writing by the grave.
  Seldom people come, except for some,
    But no one dares to speak or wave.

This is a place, many don't want to face,
    It has a quiet, solemn, final air.
  There is no feeling, or meaning, of color or race,
    All are the same, except for one name, or a pair.

God gave, He took away, forever to stay
    With Him if they followed His will.
  Not for the dead, but the living instead, we pray
    That they, humbly bow and listen still.

Time is not mine, but Thine, it is in Thy hand,
    Nothing can I change, the decision was made.
  His children are in His hand, in the promised land,
    Where joy and peace will never fade.

This stone is cold, others are old, they can't talk,
    But they hold memories of loved ones and of my son.
  Thirteen years today, he was taken away, from his walk,
    Sometimes it seems like a few months,
    or maybe just one.

To be here, several times a year, is for me a must,
>God shows me His grace, His riches and his wealth.
>This wealth is love, from above, with patience and trust,
>And how He is with me in joy, sickness and health.

He is my Guide, ever to abide, as I struggle and hope,
>Knowing He won't leave me, but remain at my side.
>If I should fall, He'll help when I call, teach me to cope,
>I can tell Him everything, there is nothing to hide.

So as I plan, when I can, to put these thoughts in a book,
>To help others, myself, to honor God and His name.
>To allow a glimpse into my heart, to be a part, get a closer look,
>This is my prayer, though it causes eruptions of pain.

When I've met this goal, will my soul, still seek this stone?
>Will I have this desire to meet God here year after year?
>It will always be, for me, a place where God and I are alone.
>For it is here I can face death without pain, without fear.
So thank you God this day,
>That I could stay and write and pray.

❖

July 29th, 1995

Alone among the never ending gravestones is like being in
    A quiet sea,
    There is no life that moves, not much to hear and little to
    See, but me.

There are the sounds of the birds, a few twitters or a
    Muffled song,
    They've come to comfort me, for God created us, it is to
    Him we belong.

My thoughts wander back home, Greg's old home, where
    His siblings still wander in and out.
    They bring their families and friends to visit or stay, there
    Is always someone about.

Everyone passes by Greg's pictures as they come and go, so
    Greg is there too,
    He is still very much a part of our home, like all of us, he
    Was just passing through.

Greg's passing was early, so was my mother's; the same for
    My dear friend,
    They all had more to live, much more we thought, but
    God knew it was the end.

It is hard for all of us to live each day as if it were our very
    Last,
    We would like that last day to come slowly, surely not very
    Fast.

It is times like today, here under the clouded sky, the peeking
    Sun,

That the mind can fully concentrate on God, our Maker, the
    Holy One.

We must never forget amidst the daily chores to remember
    Just why we are here,
      We are servants, taking on every small or awesome task
      Knowing God's help is near.

When I feel pressed, I sing, "Make me a servant, oh, make me
    Like You,
      For You are a Servant, make me
      One too."

It is this thought that helps me, strengthens me, makes me
    Aware,
      I cannot sit and wait to be called home; now is the time to
      Prepare.

Greg's preparations are over; his time to prepare was shorter
    Than some,
      God helped him to make ready, hard though it was, to enter
      His last home.

So why after all these years do I still shed tears and why do I
    Still grieve?
      It is because I miss Greg, I love him; it has nothing to do with
      What I believe.

I believe God is merciful and loving and took Greg because
    Of a deep love for him.
      Oh, God, help me to know Your will, for in You I can
      Never lose, only win.

So for today, I leave this serene place where God and I
    Can be alone,
      May He help me daily to retrieve these moments when
      Back in my busy home.

1996

(14 Years)

April 20ᵗʰ, 1996

On Saturday, 14 years ago today,
  we all gathered to say,
  "Good-bye our beloved Greg."

It was here amidst blossoms of cherry and dogwood,
  That I so wanted to stay, if I could,
  But only Greg was allowed to remain.

Today there is rain in the air,
  But I really don't care
  That I am getting wet.

My mind needs to wander back,
  To help fill in where I lack
  The courage to go on.

Alone here among masses of quiet graves,
  I ponder the mighty power that saves
  Souls from eternal death.

And what about others I know,
  Who mourn and it doesn't show,
  Help me to be there.

What have I learned since Greg left,
  Has it been enough, have I met
  All challenges.

How many years might still remain,
　　Will anything ever be the same,
　　The road goes on.

There must never be an end
　　To challenges around each bend,
　　It has to be that way.

Strength is overcoming, holding fast,
　　Not letting up until the very last
　　Challenge comes, death.

Greg's trials were scoreless and tough,
　　He weakened, but had just enough
　　Strength to pass the test.

God's grace was evident and I knew
　　It was given only to a chosen few,
　　Oh, what merciful love.

I need to recall, lest I forget
　　The events in Greg's death and yet
　　I must dwell now on life.

God surely needs me today, tomorrow too,
　　Maybe to help someone like you,
　　Thank you, God.

Yes, my mind needs to wander back
　　To help fill in where I lack
　　The courage to go on.

　　Help me, oh God.

❖

July 27ᵗʰ, 1996

I clean away the grass from the grave
    and set a plant to one side;
      Anyone watching surely would know why I'm here,
      it's hard to hide.

If ever I saw anyone else with a pillow, blanket,
    pencil and pad;
      Sit by a grave for hours on end and write,
      it would make me sad.

And yet I yearn for these moments,
    for this peaceful, quiet time,
      To ponder death, but also to reflect on life,
      Greg's life and mine.

Birthdays, too, are never forgotten
    even for those no longer here,
      So this is Greg's day; it will always be filled
      with memories of fun and cheer.

I had to come here to talk with God;
    I was drawn away from home;
      Some day you may understand,
      but for now I am here all alone.

In some ways it gets easier;
    but at times the load is still hard to bear;
      If you have walked this road,
      then these thoughts with you I share.

Some feelings never change,
    the ones so close and deep in the heart;

They are in safe keeping even when
   you and the one you love are apart.

And then on a day like today they surface,
   just like they were new;
They allow the soul to refocus on life,
   so as to get a better view.

May God grant each one the vision,
   the ability to see it all so clear;
To understand why He calls some home,
   while the rest wait here.

There is still so much to learn, to know;
   how long will it all take?
I pray the Lord will be gracious
   for there are many souls at stake.

My purpose is different from Greg's, from yours,
   or that of my friend;
God knows when our purpose is completed,
   when our lives will end.

May God never leave us, but stay,
   At your side and mine until that day.

1997

(15 Years)

April 21ˢᵗ, 1997

Twenty years ago Greg left the land of his birth, the only place
    he knew;
    To come to America, a place of dreams, of which Greg
        had more than a few.

His dreams were not only for himself, but for all who touched
    his life;
    He went the extra mile to seek a perfect way to bring joy,
        even in strife.

God knew each dream, but had to change a few; Greg would
    understand why;
    It was best that Greg didn't know so soon that he would
        have to die.

When the moment was right and Greg's heart was ready
    for the test;
    God gave him time to answer each question before he allowed
        him to rest.

Some answers must have been hard to find, or maybe he really
    didn't want to know;
    But the test had to be completed, time was fleeting;
        why couldn't it just go slow.

Did Greg get all the answers right; what will it be, the
    final score?
    What if he left out an important part, or a word or
        two or more?

How does God grade His tests, on a curve or each
     to his own?
    God will call, one by one, to come to Him and there
     to stand alone.

Those who pass the test will hear, "Well done; enter
     in, My son."
    It is by God's mercy and grace that Greg endured,
     passed and won.

This is not a quiet place on this cool, brisk
     April day;
    A gravedigger prepares for a burial in his own
     routine way.

Death has come to another and death has no
     plan to cease;
    It races with time and wins, because death knows
     no real peace.

Death separates body and soul, for many it may
     mean the end;
    Only memories will remain of a loved one or of
     a dear friend.

For God's children, death is the channel to God's
     dwelling place;
    Into the home of souls, a home for the faithful who
     finished the race.

Thank you, God, for salvation, for victory over death
     and its hold;
    For allowing Greg and all your chosen ones to safely
     enter the fold.

Life now calls me away, once again I
     must leave.
    O, God, help me daily my spiritual goals
     to achieve.

August 28ᵗʰ, 1997

Do years stop tears after someone you love
    is gone?

Some say time erases
    the grief.

For me neither is true, where do
    I belong?

With those who don't
    seek relief?

But Why?

Reminders of the deep, empty spaces
    of the heart,

Teach me the uncertainty of the life
    given to live,

Understand God's grace, though surely
    only in part,

Accept His love in Greg's death
    and to give.

But Why?

Learning about God must be more than words
    on book's pages,

Is it here at the grave where the wind rustles
    through my hair?

Or in His creation, His children, His love down
    through the ages,

Is it in the death of a dear one that truly
    makes me aware?

But Why?

Feeling alone makes me reach to the One Who
    is always the same,

My Guide, my Helper, my Strength, my Hope, my
    Savior, my Rock;

It is God Who knows me, knows the length of my wait
    until He calls my name.

So, death does teach me about life, about what I must
    learn and how to walk.

That's why!

It is dusk, so,
        I must go.

1998

(16 Years)

Though this passageway meanders through the valley of the shadow of death where danger lurks at every bend, those who keep stride with God fear no evil. Like a loving Shepherd He guides His flock into the fold, into His glory, forever. He is the King of glory; thanks be unto Him.

❖

April 11th, 1998

Do you have a place
  Where thoughts of the world are few?
 Seek this place; seek it in haste,
  For it is somewhere waiting for God and you.

Some look for a room,
  possibly behind a closed door,
 Or the stillness of a river
  or the top of a peak;
 Others go to a church building
  and kneel to the floor,
 While a few don't yet know where
  they and God will meet.

Maybe it is by the hearth
  when all in the house are at rest,
 Or where you can look to the stars
  from a window seat,
 Or on the porch at night
  where the cat warms her loving guest,
 You will find a place,
  it will be your place where you and God meet.

Now when you find your place
      it will be open day and night,
   Not just when you have a burdensome heart
      or stumbling feet,
  But also when you want to say, "Thank you"
     or make things right,
   Because it is your own place;
      the place where you and God meet.

I have many places where I talk to God
     and they are all mine,
   But the place I like best is at my son's grave,
     it is just for me.
  No one calls me and yet it is like
     I have my own open line,
   A line to God, direct, with no limits
     and it is always free.

It is free because God has graciously chosen me
     as His own,
   He engulfs me in His creation
     so beautiful, perfect and complete.
 And yet this is only a taste of His heavenly home,
     my home,
   Yes, I yearn to come here,
     I am in awe that God and I can meet.

The cold wind tries to keep the sun
     from warming my ears.
   April colors are vibrant
     though the grass is muddy and wet.
  This is Greg's month,
     God freed him from his pain and tears.
   Greg knew where he was going,
     for He and God had often met.

The time for everyone will come,
  death chooses each one.
 But I will never be alone,
   and with God there is no fear of defeat.
 Death will not pass over me, I too will die;
   I will see my son.
 I know my heart is heard,
   here where God and I meet.

❖

July 29ᵗʰ, 1998

A mist falls, a bird calls,
    Stillness settles within the walls.

The sky is gray, on this,
    Greg's day,
        The sun sneaks in a golden ray.

His body is at rest after many a test,
    His soul is at home, God knows best.

Distant thunder makes me wonder,
    Of God's power to save or tear asunder.

Flowers in a basket, flowers for a casket,
    A new plot touches Greg's, can't get past it.

A lawn mower disturbs, almost perturbs,
    He nods, whispers "Hi," no other words.

Bodies die and come here to lie,
    Does he ever think to ask why?

The grave was never meant to save,
    Salvation is through the Son God gave.
Yes I know, I must go,
    For the sun is getting low.

But I do want to keep this retreat,
    Where God and I can always meet.

❖

April 21ᵗʰ, 1999

(17 Years)

At the Grave

Was it yesterday, was it today?
    Or was it seventeen years ago?
It is so often very hard to say,
    Things at the grave change so slow.

The same trees still bloom,
    Cherry blossoms pink and white;
Birds sing their familiar tune,
    It makes things seem so right.

God planned this world. He knew
    Its importance would someday fade;
Eternal things were in His view,
    Long ago when this earth was made.

But yet, I am still sad,
    Why must it be this way?
At the same time my heart is glad
    That Greg has gone home to stay.

Yesterday youths lost their lives
    By the guns of only two,
A whole nation weeps and cries,
    My heart also goes out to you.

So quickly one can snuff a life out,
    No time to prepare, no time to run.
The day had begun like others, no doubt,
    Until deep despair darkened the sun.

With Greg, God gave us time,
>We knew his days would be few.
>It was God's way, His design,
>>What will it be for me, for you?

Life is uncertain, that is for sure,
>For the young, the old, for all;
>It is our faith that helps us endure,
>>Make us ready for when You call.

And for my children and their own,
>Dear God, may I humbly ask;
>Prepare them for their heavenly home,
>>Help them complete each task.

As You have been my Strength and Shield,
>So may You be to them, each one;
>That they may learn to seek You first, to yield;
>>And say, "My God, let Thy will be done."

Rain has come, it is wet, I must depart.
>The lawn mower nears Greg's grave;
>Oh, God, please watch over my heart.
>>Make me a servant, keep me brave.

❖

July 29ᵗʰ, 1999
At the Grave

The graveyard is fresh and clean,
 The sun is going down,
  Some quiet wanderers can be seen,
   Just getting away from the busy town.

They don't know why I sit, why I write,
 To ask would be rather rude,
  They just enjoy the beauty while it is light,
   It is hard for them to sense my mood.

The day started early, getting grandchildren to wake,
 It was time to get dressed and down to eat,
  Other children arrive, no one wanted to be late,
   Curling irons, happiness and white socks on the feet.

This day is Greg's birthday, the children didn't know,
 Inside, I remembered, a mother can never forget,
  Costumes and karaoke were loaded for the show,
   It was their day, too, I had to keep in step.

Greg loved music and would have been so proud,
 His nieces and nephew got the songs down pat.
  They sang at the adult center, strong and loud,
   His nephew wore his old Swiss top and black hat.

Now, God, You know why I came,
 You know what I needed to do,
  You know that life is never the same,
   When someone you love is with You.

The older I get
The more I understand
And yet,
I still miss Greg.

My mind understands,
But,
My heart commands,
I still miss Greg.

Somehow though,
God helps me
To know
It's OK to miss Greg.

B.

WRITINGS OF GREG'S FAMILY

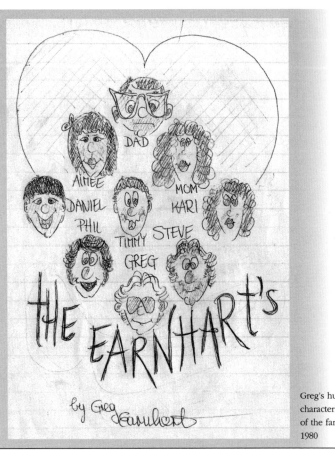

Greg's humorous
characterization
of the family
1980

6

A FAMILY REMEMBERS

The following writings were penned by Greg's own personal family, the family he knew would never leave him. He knew, however, he would have to leave them.

Greg's puzzle as a mother sees it.

Greg's life was like a puzzle.

It was a game of patience.
It was a test of skills and ingenuity.
It was at times a bewilderment and a mystery.
It was the putting together of many scattered pieces.
It was in the hands of One who placed the first corner piece,

Then carefully, additional pieces were placed as they fit.
Finally finished, it allowed the full picture to be revealed.

It was like a masterful piece of art.
It was ready to go to a secure place.
It was ready to join other masterpieces.
It was taken to its final place of honor.
It is in the palace of the Master Himself, forever.

❖

August 18th, 1981

An excerpt from a newsletter written by Greg's father

Letters pour in daily expressing concern and inquiring about Greg. After a strenuous week at camp we are trying to get back in the harness here at home. Greg stood up under the rather hectic schedule at camp surprisingly well. To the amazement of all he even participated in a most lively skit for the talent show. Obviously, he has made dramatic improvement since the eleven-day hospitalization in July when the doctors fought to save him from a near lethal first round of chemotherapy. Greg's positive and trusting attitude is decidedly in his favor. We are lifted up by the mercy of God in the hope He provides and thank all of you for your prayers and expressions of love and concern. Continue to pray with us.

From Greg's brother-in-law given after Greg's death

The following is something that I wrote last year, the summer of 1981. Shortly after we found out that Greg had cancer I felt something inside that had to be dealt with. This poem is my way of dealing with my fear of what has happened to Greg:

Why must life look this way to me now
When my future had so much to give,
Why can't this trouble pass, and let me live?
I have many things I'd like to do
So many places left to explore,
Why can't this pass, and reopen the door?
Life came to me in a blink of an eye,
Now moments later life is beginning to pass,
My hope is growing weaker, I can't last.
The pain that I feel deep inside of me
Is simply more than I can take,
I keep hoping it's all a dream, but I don't wake.
All that I need is some help to cope
With this overburdening ordeal,
I know it's a reality, I just don't know what to feel.
So please, help me, there's so little I understand,
So just stand near, and hold my hand.
Time has nothing to offer me
But more pain and sorrow to bear,
My dreams had just reached fulfillment,
Suddenly they disappeared in the air.
My rainbow has been fading for many unknown years,
Though I still hold to the bow, the pot of gold has disappeared.
I have little to recognize as the person I once was

Just some bones and flesh, living only because
Of the love I've received from you and the hope you've
    held for me
You've lightened my burden all the way
Thanks to you there is some light to see.

I think you can see that I was hoping for a different ending than reality gave us. But which ending proves more profitable? The ordeal is over, the pain is gone and the burden has been lifted. We always pray that God's will be done, and it has, for all of us. With most sincere love.

❖

MEMORIES, Spring 1983
Written to Greg by his older sister

One could fill a lifetime just with memories alone and it is these memories that keep you alive within me.

I was only six years old when you came into my life, but how well I remember. Of course, you immediately became the center of attention and it did not take you very long before you had us all figured out. But the one you wrapped around your little finger was your Grandma Dorothy, a very special lady. When she went back to America you were no fun to have around and I am not sure who missed her more, you or I. One word comes to mind to explain your behavior—spoiled.

I kept waiting for that white "peach fuzz" that resembled hair to turn brown, but you fooled me and I decided that blond was your color. I often wondered if you did that intentionally just to get more attention wherever you went, because you certainly succeeded. Everyone always thought you were so cute and were wanting to know where you got that blond hair.

You never lacked in the entertainment field, everything from sleepwalking to clown acts to puppet shows and circus performances. You always had me on the edge of my seat, rolling in laughter.

When you were eight I remember you wanting to know whether or not you were adopted. I guess it was your blond hair and very blue eyes that got you to question your heritage, but looking a little different from the rest of us is what made you so special.

As you grew older you never lacked in having friends, and your friends became my friends. Watching you with them taught me what true friendships were all about. You had a special gift in relating to them and your thoughts and emotions went deeper than anyone could have imagined. You had a big "heart" and you got your feelings hurt easily. That must have been why you packed your bags more than once and a few times succeeded in leaving home. And then, upon returning from your short adventure, would try to hide behind a book as you ate your meal, thinking you would not be noticed! The food always brought you back because you never missed a meal.

We shared so many fun times together, and even though the two of us argued a lot, it brought us closer together. When I went off to college, I came to a sudden realization that we were growing up and I wondered if the fun times we had had would ever be the same again. But there was no need to worry because once I was home from college we again were a team. Remember all those nights you faithfully accompanied me to my night classes when it was hard to stay awake because the teacher was so boring? And then the night when we got pulled over by a policeman for speeding? We laughed so hard because in all the confusion he didn't write us up a ticket.

Life continued to be everything but boring; you made sure of that. Planning for the holidays and surprise birthday parties were always so much fun because I could count on you to make magical things happen. You were magic and with it you brightened the lives of so many in so many different ways

When you left me, a part of me left with you. Without you, life for me took on a new meaning, a more serious one. The magic was gone and I found it harder to have fun and to laugh and to be free of worries and sad thoughts. But life is too short to dwell on the "whys" and "why nots," so as the wounds are slowly healing within me I find myself once again enjoying each day for what it brings and living it to the fullest, always remembering how much you enjoyed life and everything it stood for.

I still miss the magic and I miss you, but I am so thankful for the years we did have and were allowed to share together as a brother and sister, as a very special team. Thank you, Greg.

❖

October 1985
"CHANGE"

Written by Greg's youngest brother, age 13 for an English class

A single experience brought upon an important change in me. On a Wednesday night at 9:30 p.m. with my family surrounding his bed, my second oldest brother, Greg, age 18, died of cancer. Greg got the cancer when he was in the musical, *Oklahoma!*. Part of his act was to fall on his knee and jump back up. Well, this led to cancer in the knee, then it spread to the lungs.

After his death I thought to myself, boy, how neat to have a brother who fought for life. He never gave up and said, "Oh well, I'm going to die, might as well give up." He always struggled, hoping that he would live. He always went to school even when he was sick.

It wasn't but a year later when I found out that I had a tumor in my knee too; I guess it runs in the family. I thought to myself, will I die like Greg? Will I have to experience pain, suffering and more? In a few months I had surgery and it was taken out. I had no troubles until this summer when it began to hurt again. I hope it's not growing back. The main thing that changed in me was to challenge whatever lies ahead of me.

❖

March, 1990

It was musical time at the high school and Oklahoma! *was the chosen script. The winter before, when the actors were being cast, the directors wanted Greg's youngest brother for a supporting role. Greg's mother asked the directors to please pick a different musical and use* Oklahoma! *after her youngest had graduated; the memories of Greg would be too overwhelming. The directors, however, felt they had the perfect cast for the chosen script and suggested dedicating it to Greg. And so it was. With Greg's youngest brother wearing the same black hat Greg wore some nine years earlier, the musical,* Oklahoma!, *was dedicated to Greg.*

Dedication:
GREGORY DEAN EARNHART
1963–1982

This is not the first *Oklahoma!* that has been presented here at the high school. The musical was performed in the spring of 1981 and among the cast was a hard-working and talented boy, Greg Earnhart. In addition to rehearsal, Greg designed, helped build and painted the set. He also created the posters for the show.

Six weeks before his senior graduation, cancer took Greg's life. Greg's brother, along with the cast and crew would like to dedicate this 1990 production to him.

❖

January 29ᵗʰ, 1993
"He Slipped Through The Cracks That Night"
Written by Greg's youngest brother

It was a typical evening around our house. In fact, nothing out of the ordinary was really happening. Dad was on his way home from the office, and Mom was in the kitchen reviving last night's leftovers. If you stepped outside you would find the temperature to be mild, a slight nip in the air, and dusk quickly on its way. I had been running around the house looking for something to do. I was bored. I was twelve. And I was hungry.

It seemed as if this Wednesday in April was rapidly going down in history as any other Wednesday in the Earnhart household. We always had the same routine: we all sat down for some type of meal right at six-o-clock, and then prepared ourselves for Wednesday night Bible study which began at 7:30 at the church building. We would all return home, find our respected areas throughout the large two-story house and pretty much hibernate until bedtime. Every once in a while something would drastically change those plans. And if you kept track of what usually would go differently, it was most likely a fight between two of us kids. We were a family that did things together. We were a family that went to church together.

This particular Wednesday in April, things went differently. Actually things had been different around out house for quite sometime, ever since Greg, the second oldest son, had been stricken with cancer in his left knee. He was only seventeen when he acquired the cancer, but he had been fighting it like an adult. This Wednesday night Mom stayed home from church to be with Greg. He had been laid up in bed for a couple of weeks now. Over the last few months the cancer had spread to his left lung and was rapidly depleting his breath for life. Greg was a fighter. He simply wanted Mom. He needed just her this Wednesday night, that's all.

The rest of the family piled into the van at 7:15 and departed for the church building just a few miles away. Dad did not say much on the way there. I sensed something was deeply engulfing his thoughts and it seemed best that I, being the youngest, just not ask any questions.

Greg had been fighting this terrible disease for just about a year. Never once did he give up. Never once did he shed a tear for death. He loved life and wanted to live.

The drive home from church was long. At least it seemed long this time. I felt as if something evil was lurking within our van, something that everyone else seemed to feel also. I still remember that night as if it were yesterday. As I walked through the weather-torn front door, I could feel it. I wasn't sure what it was, but I felt it and I didn't like it.

Dad rushed upstairs while the rest of us kids stood at the bottom of the stairs wondering what had struck a family with so much love. I began to feel sick to my stomach. I remember going to the bathroom and trying to throw up, but I couldn't. I just stared into the toilet looking for answers, but they weren't there. I remember seeing a ripple hit the calm water that so faithfully filled the toilet. I was crying, but why? There wasn't any bad news, yet. It was probably the enormous amount of love I had for my brother, and it was slowly being torn away.

Dad returned to the head of the staircase and asked that we all come up to Greg's bedroom. I had gone up and down these stairs a million times. I knew there were thirteen steps and the fourteenth at either end meant you had reached the top or had glided off the last one at the bottom. I had even taken them three at a time, but tonight I didn't even want to start up that first one.

I rounded the corner into his bedroom, took a few painful steps and saw my brother lying in his bed. He looked comfortable, but I knew the pain to him was unbearable. I remember my mom sitting on his bed leaning up against the wall. She looked tired and her face was wet with tears. I saw Greg reach out his hand for my father's comfort. It brought great joy to see that he was still grasping for life.

Dad crouched down next to the bed, held Greg's hand and began to pray. All of us kids were holding each other by now. I remember my oldest sister, the oldest in the family, clutched me to her as if I was a soft teddy bear wanting a hug. It was quiet. The rain could be heard pecking at the window. The whispers of Dad's voice coated every wall around us. The only light cast across the room was coming from Greg's desk. Seconds seemed like hours, and hours like days.

We all were given a chance to say good-bye to our brother of eighteen years. This time he wouldn't be coming home on that bright yellow school bus. This time Dad wouldn't go pick him up from soccer practice. This time he wouldn't be coming home late from play practice, tired and ready for some supper. He wouldn't even get into the family van for one last trip to the green church building that sat on the corner of 2nd and Juniper. This time he would go to a place where the pain would cease forever. He had conquered his enemy. He had won the battle. He was going home to celebrate.

As he lay there asleep, forever, I took one last look at the friend I had met and grown to love over the many years we spent together in the house on the corner of 14th and Oak. He was a legend in my heart and a brother through Christ, who had died on the cross. He made me realize that each day has a new sunrise and each dusk has a different sunset. He was, and always will be, the only one who ever taught me the real meaning of life.

❖

July, 1997
Written by Greg's youngest sister

My memories of Greg are in the ways in which he brought us closer together as a family. Like the time Greg set up a store in his bedroom closet door to tempt us with toys, chewing gum and other
knickknacks. My brothers and I would scrounge up pennies and
quarters so we could bargain with his prices. Imagine having a store
in our own home. What a great community.

❖

June 1997
"Make Me Cry"
Written by Greg's younger brother

It was on a Wednesday evening after we had come home from Bible
class that I helped Greg down the narrow hallway to the bathroom.
One had to partially carry him while holding on to the oxygen tank
that needed to follow along to help Greg breathe. The lungs were
so full with tumors that his breathing in the last few weeks had
become very weak. He seemed to have little strength this evening.
I had a strange feeling that Greg might be taking the last steps of
his life on earth. I helped him back into bed and then rushed down
to tell Mom that I thought Greg was not doing well at all. He was
not responding as he usually did.

It was not long after Mom went into Greg's room that she came
back out to call the family together. My older sister and brother
came over so that the whole family could be together one more
time. We gathered in his room and sat quietly as Mom continued to

talk to him. We could do nothing but stare at him for what looked to be the last time. A few short minutes later, as if Greg waited until all the family was together, his spirit peacefully left his body.

The tears began to flow like the waters of the Columbia River, except for mine. "Why am I not crying?" I asked myself. If there ever was a moment that I really wanted to cry, this was it. To this day I could not say why I ended up having to force myself to cry. Was it that I knew that Greg would not want us to shed a tear over his death? Was it that I knew that Greg was really not leaving us at all, that he was just waiting for us to meet him again? Was it because he had left such a good impression in people's lives, that he will live on in others? Or was it because I knew that missing him would hold me back from reaching forward to tomorrow? Reaching for tomorrow by taking the steps of opportunities today, propels one to overcome the most difficult adversaries.

Greg never slowed down mentally even while his body slowed to a crawl. He pursued every day in hope of making a difference in someone else's life. He gave of himself to his last breath.

Greg, I will see you soon.

C.

WRITINGS OF GREG'S FRIENDS

7

KINDRED SPIRITS
AROUND THE GLOBE

W E WERE NEVER ALONE in this "chapter" of Greg's life. There were hundreds of loved ones and friends who walked with us through each page. Not everyone's personal feelings of the heart were written to the family, though expressions thereof were communicated in numerous other ways. Every outreach has been gratefully accepted, appreciated and still remembered. Greg's support groups encompassed him to the end, as hand-in-hand they stretched around the world. Those blessings, once bestowed, continue to multiply even today.

This chapter is composed of excerpts from only a few of the many letters of friends, teachers, town folks and loved ones, young and old. It is for all who wish to remember the sincere sentiments that surrounded Greg's illness and death. His memories linger on in different ways, in each one of those who knew him best.

written by a choreographer of Oklahoma!

To Greg:
The first day at rehearsal,
  You all had two left feet;
  You couldn't keep the rhythm,
  And you couldn't feel the beat.

But time went on; my hopes were raised,
  You really did O.K.
  And by opening performance,
  You were really on your way.

So, when you're asked to do a thing,
  Don't say, "Oh, I don't know."
  Remember March of '81,
  And the Oklahoma! show.

And, thank you just for being "You",
  It's been a real delight,
  May all your life be filled with joy,
  Just the way you feel tonight!

The following segments are from Greg's high school friends

Greg and I became friends our sophomore year in art class. In the time that followed we worked together on most of the musicals and plays as well as other projects. I still remember the warm, sunny day last year when we took a backdrop outside to paint for the May Day program, and had great fun walking around barefooted. In the two and a half years that I have known Greg, he became one of my closest friends. I just wanted you to know how glad I am that I have known Greg. I am not likely to forget the fun we have had together. I share in your sorrow. May God help you through these hard times.

Two and a half years later this same friend wrote:

I still miss Greg a lot, especially during rough times. I've had a lot of those this past year. It helps to think of what Greg would have said to me and I like to think he is somewhere talking to me even though I can't hear him. He was a good friend then and is a good friend even now.

This is to tell you how much Greg helped me. Greg showed so much courage and love, as well as a Christian attitude, that it just made me even more eager to become closer to the Lord.

Greg was a good friend and helped me in ways he didn't even know. I am going to miss him, but I know he is better off now and I will see him again.

I just want to apologize for neglecting to share something with you at the funeral service of your son. I was rather speechless when you greeted me. I am now a student in Salem and it was here that I received news of Greg's death. I was shocked at what seemed to me the swiftness of his illness. My buddies here noticed that I was deeply troubled, so we all got down and cried out to God on your behalf. I am very thankful for Greg's commitment to God, for it is through this, in Greg's death, that some five guys here were raised up with a fervent zeal to serve God and continue the work that was started in Greg. I mourn with you in your son's death, but I also rejoice in God's goodness to us. I know God will bless you.

Townsfolk express their thoughts

Life is much like a beautiful tree
    It's the living branches that we see.

And the roots that are hidden strong and deep
    Are the beautiful memories our hearts may keep.

I would like Greg's goodness and gentleness to be remembered, as we remember him.

❖

My thoughts and prayers are with you. We will all miss Greg; he touched everyone in a very special way and made my life richer with his friendship.

Greg was a great friend that I have never forgotten. The thing that sticks with me more than anything; he just never seemed to stop smiling. I'll never forget that.

We want to extend to you our sympathy over the loss of your son Greg. He was a valiant young man in his days of suffering. He was an example to many of us in his Christian life. His attitude and life experiences will give his fellow classmates and many of us greater hope and a reinforcement of the meaning of "faith." We support you in your loss with our prayers.

I am sure you know how much Greg was loved by all who knew him. He was a beautiful person and especially during this past year, displaying so much courage and tranquillity in facing his illness. He was an inspiration to us all and we are grateful for having had his friendship.

Greg wrote this note to a friend on the program of his first musical,
The Sound of Music:

You're a real nice and sweet person, hope you stick around for
the next few years.

This friend's response sometime after Greg's death:

I remember thinking how unfair life was. Here I took drugs, ran
away and wanted to die. Greg had so much to give the world, yet
he was dying. My thinking was changed by Greg's experience.
I quickly put a greater value on my life and on other people's lives.

A high school newspaper staff member remembers

I can't tell you how sorry I am about Greg passing away. He was a
good friend to me in the time that I knew him and he was a joy to
have on the newspaper staff.

Greg was an inspiration to everyone on the staff, mainly
because he always kept calm, even when it seemed that the walls
were caving in around us. His calmness was always like a blanket
being laid over the staff and we would all soon be "back to normal."
We always knew that if we got into a scrape we could just run to
him asking for a cartoon and he would gladly make one up, no
complaints. I can't remember how many times he literally saved us
from having a big blank spot on a page.

My advisor and I sat down and discussed what we could do in
Greg's memory. He suggested writing a story on Greg's life, but that
idea just didn't seem quite right to me. So, I did what I thought Greg
would have wanted me to do, something artistic that would bring

pleasure to others. I realized right away that I didn't have the talent it would take to draw the front page, so I used all of the past cartoons that he had done for us.

Although they all hold memories for me there is one cartoon in particular that I have always loved; it's the one at the top of the front page of the paper I'm giving to you. There is a man on a deserted island, a ship pulls up and asks directions to New York. The man points the way and the ship sails off leaving the man behind.

The reason I love this cartoon so much is because it was a last minute job for Greg. I was really in a bind and needed his help. When he brought the cartoon in to me, he didn't want to let me see it and he kept holding it to his body. He kept saying it over and over, "I'll let you see it, but you have to promise not to laugh 'cause it's stupid, it's not even funny." He finally let me see it after I promised I wouldn't laugh, but unfortunately the cartoon struck me as being funny and I couldn't keep my promise. I laughed and laughed and laughed.

Well, Greg turned beet red and kept saying, "You're just trying to make me feel good, come on, knock it off. I know it's not funny so you don't have to laugh." He never did believe that I really liked that cartoon.

By now it's probably pretty obvious to you that I miss Greg a lot, but I feel better knowing that he is with the Lord in heaven. I sincerely hope you like the front page. I'm sorry that I couldn't do any more, but I'm just not very artistic. I always left the art up to Greg.

CLASS OF 1982

April 1982

written by a drama teacher at the high school

I would like to express to you my feelings of love for all of you during this eternal lapse of time.

I refer to an "eternal lapse of time" because I am never ceased to be amazed and cleansed that when God calls one of our beloved it is always as if we become caught, so to speak, in time. I immediately stop my daily mental processes and reflect on the sights and sounds and all senses that God has arranged beautifully for each of us in so many striking ways. The multicolored greens of spring that shelter and shade us, the vivid yellow, red, purple tulip shape configurations that we smiled at yesterday, the glimpse of a squirrel leaping from tree to tree, the joy of discovering again a new songbird in the area. There are the simple quiet reminders of life here on earth and the tell-tale signs of an amazing God! I could, not on the confines of this paper, begin to list all of this presence of God. But I would like to share with you some of my personal recollections and moments about Gregory Dean Earnhart.

I love you, Greg, and I always shall. Never have I been so blessed to have worked alongside such a dedicated and talented human being as Greg. He was persistent, beautifully stubborn, and tremendously effective at finishing the final touches of a theater set design. He would walk to the back of our auditorium and say, "I'm not sure if I like it, but please tell your 4th period students not to paint in the wrong colors in the areas I've indicated." Later, Greg was usually quietly there on the set by himself, finishing up. A smile would appear and he would state that the set was going to turn out OK after all. But that was only after every detail was worked out. Also, that information was imparted quietly to myself. Greg was not much for fanfare. He was quietly effective. How he used his God-given talents!

The quality of love is probably the most single important influence in all of our lives. There is in our lives a multi-experience of love for our children, love for our parents, love for our brothers and sisters and love for a friend. The nurturing that we receive from our mothers and fathers is to me the single most important influence in our lives. It is that caring that I saw was so evident in Greg's life. What a beautiful compliment to you, the parents of Greg, and to Greg for the love you shared with each other.

There is one particular account of a moment that Greg and I dealt with that I would like to share with you. I feel it was special and maybe a sign of God working behind the scenes. There was a brief interlude of an objection with the content of the play which I respected then and still respect today. I feel I had made an honest, sincere, attempt to deal with this matter. However, I was aware of the seriousness of the matter on a parental decision of Greg not being able to participate. I've always respected this matter and I want you to know I was grappling with this problem the best way I knew how. In any event I went to school and on my path to my classroom I chose a route which I never travel merely because it was out of my way. I came across Greg standing at the lower end of "B" hall by the west wing. He was not even focusing on anyone, but I could tell by his look that he felt like he was searching for an answer. I said, "Greg, I'm sorry if I'm wrong and if you like I'll do anything you want,…just tell me what." I knew just looking at Greg that this was a most important event in this chapter of his life. Greg only apologized for being such a problem. We agreed that we would meet in my room during break to discuss the matter. Later, before the break, I made the decision to talk to another director to discuss with Greg's father to take out of the play whatever was necessary.

During break, Greg and I met in the back of my room. I informed him that he was going to be in the play, that changes were being made and tears came to his eyes. By nature, I am a very sensitive person. I said, "Greg, I just want you to know that you are one of my heroes!" I remember both of us crying. I also know there was a touch of God sitting with us and discussing that morning in lower "B."

Greg went on to play some very memorable performances. He was extremely funny in his scenes and I remember discussing his believable character in theater class.

Thursday April 22, I arrived at school to find a small piece of yellow paper attached to our sign-in sheet. It read, "last night at 10 p.m. we lost Greg Earnhart." It was at that moment that time seemed to stop. Later during 2nd period, my theater class and I sat in desks, tears were shed and we all shared together that "eternal lapse of time." I remember going over to a little girl who was crying and sat on her desk and put my arm around her. In a very troubled voice I talked about all the positive moments that Greg had shared with us. I wanted to share with the class the example of talent and responsibility that Greg demonstrated to all of us. I wanted them to know how wonderful it was to have known Greg within our lifetime. Then we looked at pictures of Greg that we realized were now very special and traced back all of the posters of plays that Greg had drawn.

Today, Mr. and Mrs. Earnhart, I saw you at school. I embraced you and I cried; I miss Greg. I shall miss his presence and his contributions, but I shall never forget what he stood for.

"I love you, Greg." My love to you all.

Because Greg spoke German/Swiss the first fourteen years of his life he was remembered in the hearts of those who watched him grow up. The following words share the thoughts of many cards and letters.

"Nichts darf uns trennen, Herr, von dir, nicht Angst, nicht Trübsal oder Leiden; nichts, was uns sonst begegnet hier, kann uns von deiner Liebe scheiden." In dieser Stunde der Trauer und des Leides sind wir in Gedanken und im Gebet bei Euch. Möge Gott Euch Kraft und Trost schenken.

"Nothing can separate us from the love of Christ, not fear or tribulation or distress, or things present or things to come." In this hour of sadness and grief we are with you in thought and prayer. May God give you strength and comfort.

Von ganzen Herzen möchten wir teilnehmen an Eurem Verlust. Wir haben von Greg's Heimgang gehört und wollen auf diesem Wege zeigen das wir an Euch denken in dieser schweren Zeit. Der Herr gebe Euch Seinen Trost durch die lebendige Hoffnung des Evangeliums, das Ihr uns in Europa verkündigt habt.

From the depths of our hearts we want to share in your loss. We have heard about Greg's passing and in this way we want to show you that we are thinking of you during this difficult time. May the Lord give you His comfort through the living hope of the gospel, which you proclaimed to us in Europe.

D.

WRITINGS OF GREG

Self Portrait

Junior at
Canby High
School

8

IN GREG'S OWN WORDS

Greg kept a journal and wrote in it almost every day. It wasn't until after his death that those nearest to him looked into its pages. Several pages were gone and the ten months he dealt with cancer were incomplete. It was assumed because of the missing pages that he didn't want anyone to know how he really felt or suffered. He would not have wanted to hurt or burden those he loved unnecessarily. His wishes needed to be granted.

MY JOURNAL

GREG EARNHART

September 14th, 1978

There are all kinds of smiles that brighten our world every day of the year.

There are smiles that say, "hello," smiles that say, "I care,"
And smiles that reveal much more than words can ever say.

❖

September 21ˢᵗ, 1978

Written about 16 months after Greg's move from Switzerland

Dear Sun,

I wanted to write you a long time ago, but I could never find the time to do so. But now I just finished my homework, and I don't have to do anything else. One thing I want to tell you is that I'm homesick. I wish I could go back to Switzerland, back to the little village of Wabern where we used to live. I would like to go back to my old friends, the apartment, all that snow, the beautiful Alps, the frozen lakes and back to the Swiss people.

Can you help me?

Oh, please do,

You are my only friend!

❖

October 4ᵗʰ, 1978
"Playing"

Running, jumping,
Talking, singing,
Playing is a fun thing to do,
Children do it,
Adults do it, and you and I do it too.

❖

The following are notes from Greg's journal not long before the cancer was diagnosed, but obviously already working in his body.

Poems written by Greg
Jan–Feb. 1981

Friendship
    You and me
    Loving, helping each other
    Everyday
    Sharing, relating
    Why doesn't the world understand?

Fly
    You and me,
    Floating, waving,
    Through outer space by night.
    Dreaming, flying with the wind,
    Only the sky is the limit.

❖

Monday Feb. 9th, 1981

I'm surprised that I even got out to first period today because I really feel awful. First of all I didn't get to bed until really late last night and because I felt so sick I had the worst dreams all night long. The weird thing is the fact that I almost never get headaches, but today my head feels like it's about to fall off.

❖

Sunday March 1st, 1981

This is really disgusting; I'm sick again!! This is the third time I've had this cold and it's driving me up the walls. The problem of course is the musical (*Oklahoma!*); I can't get any sicker. In order to get rid of it, my mom says that I need more sleep!

Well… Man, what does she expect! I have rehearsal until eleven o'clock or so then she expects me to get well? All I can hope for is that I don't get any sicker until after the musical is over.

❖

March 4th, 1981

I don't believe it; here it is only one day before our first performance. Yesterday we had a double matinee; I don't think I have ever
been so tired in my whole life. I must say though, that today I feel
like a vegetable. I'm not really tired, but I have absolutely no strength
and I'm almost too worn out to sit here and write.

❖

March 6th, 1981

Well tonight will be our 2nd performance and I'm already scared
now. I wasn't scared before I got the part of Slim [Greg stepped into
this part at the last minute due to a cast member's illness], but now
my stomach and throat hurts, just simply because I'm all uptight. All
of my relatives are coming tonight and some of them aren't exactly
into theater, so I hope that they like it.

❖

March 8th, 1981

After the show a lot of people commented on the scenery and the
whole show itself. I'm just a little bit mad at myself because I didn't
get enough sleep to get rid of my cold, so I didn't do all that good
on my solo. Anyway, I just hope that there is a part in the next year's
musical for me in which the notes in the song aren't so high.
    Note: The next year he had fluid on his lungs and had to be
    replaced in his role in The Fiddler on the Roof. *He died about*
    5 weeks later.

The following are letters Greg personally wrote to a very dear friend of his.

❖

June 7ᵗʰ, 1981
About a week before Greg's cancer was diagnosed

Everything else would be great around here if it weren't for my knee and my job. You see when I was in *Oklahoma!,* I was in this fight scene and kept on falling on my right knee. Well, I didn't think anything of it until my knee started to hurt about a month later. I thought that it would go away but, no, after two weeks it started to bother me to the point that I had to limp down the hallway. So I went to the doctor and he gave me some drugs. Well, the pain went away, but as soon as I ran out of drugs it started to act up again, so the doc said to take them for another week. The problem of course is that any kind of job is at stake right now and I don't have a penny to my name. Well, anyways, I hope you are enjoying your summer and I guess I'll see you at camp.

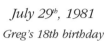

July 29ᵗʰ, 1981
Greg's 18th birthday

You'll have to excuse the messy writing, but I just so happen to be writing you this in the car. You see, we have to drive up to the hospital every weekday for radiation and that's what we're doing right now.

I'm not sure if you knew this, but I was in the hospital for one and a half weeks after my last chemotherapy and so I just got home this Sunday. I had a fever over 104 and I had about a hundred canker sores in my mouth, throat and throughout my intestinal track. So obviously I couldn't even open my mouth without it hurting and I couldn't eat anything for about two weeks. I lost 20 pounds, you should see me; If you thought I was skinny before, you haven't seen a living skeleton yet!!! Also, while I was in the hospital all of my hair fell out, so I'm bald. Mom bought me a wig; I absolutely hate it. It looks so fake and because it is parted on the side it looks another 100% worse. I guess you might say that I'm kind of depressed, having to think that I'll have to walk around looking stupid for my whole senior year!! So be prepared for a different Greg at camp. It'll probably take you all week to get used to me. (We're getting off the freeway here, so I'll catch Ya later, O.K.?)

I'm back, but this time I'm sitting here waiting for my radiation treatment. Well, here I am on my 18th birthday, the day that I've been looking forward to for a long time, but for some reason the effect has kind of been ruined by this stupid cancer! Anyways, they'll probably have a surprise party after church tonight so we'll see.

I'm really looking forward to camp, even though I will be absolutely embarrassed for the first couple of days; it'll take some getting used to. The doctors have worked everything out so that I'll get to go to camp. I'll probably get my chemotherapy in the middle of next week, so that I will have somewhat recuperated by the time we meet you guys at camp on Sunday night. Be prepared for a shock when you see me.

❖

August 17ᵗʰ, 1981

Well, how is it going? I still can't comprehend the fact that camp is already over; it just went too fast!! I don't know about you, but I had a lot of fun and it was mostly because of you! You can't imagine how badly my hair and weight loss had affected me before camp, I'm telling you, I was very much embarrassed. I wouldn't even go out into public! But you gave me the courage and strength to overcome those embarrassing feelings and now I feel so much better about going back to school. Thank you!!!! All in all, you and many others convinced me that I wasn't just a helpless cripple and that with the help of my friends and by using my mind to overpower my body, that I could accomplish many wonderful things through the power of God.

Well I gained about 3 pounds and I got this book where it has certain exercises which are supposed to help you gain weight. I only have another 15 pounds to gain (ha, ha) That's easier said than done!

Dad is going to put me back on the car insurance, so I'm going to try driving again. Watch out, the roads aren't safe anymore.

❖

Sept. 3ʳᵈ, 1981
Greg's last letter to his friend

I'm really sorry for not writing you for such a long time. I don't know what happened, but time has really flown right past me.

Two weeks ago I got my first chemotherapy treatment with just a shot. This is the kind that makes my hair fall out, but this drug they can just shoot into me over a period of 15 minutes, so that I don't have to stay for 2 days. When I got home I was suppose to throw up, but I never did. I did feel sick though. I will get this treatment once a month for approximately 5–6 months and then my hair should slowly grow back again, hopefully. Right now I'm in the hospital for my other treatment; for this I have to stay until Saturday morning. This I will have to do once a month for the next year. These two treatments are then 2 weeks apart, so that I'll be getting one treatment every two weeks. The surgery is planned for around October 1st, but that isn't definite yet

Well, enough of that boring stuff. I went to school last week to help out with the registration and I really did have a lot of fun. I like school, that is the people and the activities after school!! I also talked to one of the drama directors and he told me what the Fall play was going to be, "*David and Lisa*". You've probably never heard of it; I hadn't either. It is about this school where kids live that have mental problems. For instance, David has this fear that he will die if someone touches him and Lisa is schizophrenic. Anyways, what I am getting at is that the director said that he would let me play one of the minor roles. I could practice in the hospital and then be all ready after surgery for the performance at the end of November. I'll be on crutches of course, but that won't matter he said, because he would just put that into my character, so I'm super excited and hopefully, I'll feel up to it after the operation.

Two days ago a friend and I went to a wig shop and I tried on some new wigs. I'm really not too satisfied with the one I've got just simply because it is too straight and thus falls down. When it is windy it does the same. Besides, the whole thing doesn't fit my face; the front looks too "poofy." It's hard to explain. Anyways I ordered a new one that I really like and I'm hoping that it gets here before labor day weekend or else I have to wear my "oldy" to the first day of school on Tuesday.

Note: The knee replacement surgery was canceled due to new tumors in Greg's lung. Though very pale and limping, he did play an impressive role in "David and Lisa", his last theatrical production. His new wig arrived too late for the first day of school, but he had fun confusing the students when he went from blond to auburn. Greg's grandmother was redheaded so the color fit perfectly in the family and looked great on Greg.

9

THE LAST WORDS OF GREG
Taken from his journal

❖

January 24ᵗʰ, 1982

This Friday I went to the hospital for a checkup because I've had this terrible cold and we took some x-rays to see what was going on. Well, we saw the x-rays and they didn't look so hot, as a matter of fact it looked pretty bad. Things in my lungs looked worse, because the cancer spots had gotten bigger and bigger. Later the doctor mentioned something to the fact that they really couldn't do much of anything anymore, except for maybe taking out my worst lung. Then maybe chemotherapy will clear what's left (but it hasn't really worked so far). Well, so there we were, not really knowing what to do and so we had to start looking for some other answers.

Well, my Mom had heard from this lady in Canby about this clinic in Mexico that has cured all types of cancers. Then my Dad remembered a man in Washington who had been there and been cured, so we called him and he told us to go as soon as possible.

There was really nothing else left to do, so here I am on my way to Mexico. If everything goes as planned I'm just supposed to be there for Monday, that way I won't miss any school. Well we'll see; something else might come up.

January 29ᵗʰ, 1981

I was going to write the outcome and results on my way home on the plane, but I didn't feel like writing. Well, not everything went as planned, because I did have to stay until Wednesday which was kind of a bummer.

>*[Here Greg writes in detail how he got from the motel in California across the border to the clinic and all the tests and exams that took place.]*

One thing they did find wrong with me was the drugs had destroyed my resistance to anything. But basically what I have to do now in terms of treatment is to take this "tonic" 4 times a day and be on a special diet. I am not supposed to use my right leg at all and I'm supposed to get lots of sleep. This of course means that I can't be in the musical and I had to give up my lead role. This did make me kind of upset, not because I'll miss all of the fun, but because that's just what I like to do. I don't know why, but I've acted and done plays and stuff since I've been really small. That's just my way of life and I really miss it. There is really "No Business Like Show Business".

❖

February 3rd, 1981

I'm really super tired today and basically it's just because I've been staying up so late to work on this stupid scholarship. I must say, that if I don't win any money, I'll have a terrible fit!!!

It's not that I think that I deserve it, but it's just that I've put in so much time and effort at a time when I really should be resting. According to my doctor I'm supposed to rest even when I'm not tired, but lately I haven't even had time to lay down when I was tired.

Anyways, I feel sorry for you if you happen to be reading this journal, because I know that this must be very boring. I'm only writing all of this junk because you are making me do it, so of course it is of a pretty bad quality. [*Here he draws a happy face.*]

Off and on I keep getting these weird chest pains and they are kind of scaring me. I've had chest pains before, but that was when my cancer was growing and so now I don't know if this is what's causing it. But the pain isn't quite the same as it once was, so maybe it's just something else. Hopefully.

This might sound kind of strange, but it's really scary to have to live this way. The thing is, whenever there is some kind of pain somewhere or a swelling on my body I automatically think that my cancer has spread again. I know that this sounds stupid, but you can really make yourself sick from worrying like that. I try not to think that way, because it just really freaks me out!!

The more I think about it the more I feel sorry for you. I sure wouldn't want to read this about a student. I'm sorry, but there's really nothing to write about because everything else gets too personal.

*The following is the letter Greg submitted to the Elks
Foundation for a scholarship.*

February 2ⁿᵈ, 1982

While growing toward adolescence in Switzerland, I dreamed of
becoming a cowboy. Much of that dreaming was with pencil in
hand, thus developing my first interests in art.

After I completed the seventh grade, our family moved to Canby
and I feel privileged to have been able to participate in the many art
programs offered at Canby High School. First, I was requested to design
and paint large letters for the hallways. Later I volunteered to serve on
the "button committee," designing various buttons used for clubs and
football games. At the end of my sophomore year I was selected to be
the new cartoonist for the school newspaper and was thus given the
opportunity to explore the arts in the world of journalism.

Wall display
in Greg's room

Most likely my most enjoyable art work was for the school
musicals and plays in which I had supporting roles. I found it very
meaningful to design the posters and programs, most importantly to

help plan, build and paint the sets for all of the productions. I not only spent innumerable hours working on these projects after school and on weekends (meeting deadlines), but also learned to get along with my fellow students and four different directors who were constantly changing their minds.

Finally, with the help of the drafting program I have become very interested in the field of drafting, more especially in the area of interior design. This field offers much variety and exciting challenges and thus I am willing to spend my time and money for such a rewarding career education. My goal is to further my knowledge and art skills at a college which specializes in drafting. With your financial help this dream could also come true.

(signed) Gregory D. Earnhart

❖

February 8th, 1982
Greg's journal continues

This most certainly is a weird day, first of all, I've been home since last Wednesday and have just realized that I am really behind in my classes. Secondly, I just had to drop all of my morning classes. This probably sounds kind of strange, I know, but for the time being I am going to have to start going to school at 12, o'clock.

I don't know, most kids would probably like this, but this means that I can't work on the musical at all, so I'm kind of depressed. You see, the stage is everything to me, be it singing, acting or working behind the scenes, I love it! But just having to sit at home is a total bore!!!!!! It's not that I don't have anything to do; yes, I should be writing my A. P. Paper, or reading for West. Civ, but you see that all comes second, so there's just nothing else to do. I am planning on helping out in that last week before performance, just so I don't go insane. My doctors will probably have a bunch of cows, but who cares?

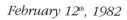

February 12th, 1982

Well, well, well, I guess I'm in a good mood today, or at least I should be in one, because of what happened yesterday. Well,

I won 2nd place in that elks scholarship contest. It really was exciting, but it was also very nerve wracking, scary and embarrassing.

We first got there and had to sit with all of the other students who were competing in this small section of this huge lodge with a dance floor, TV screen, and bar. Then they started calling us in one by one to this small conference room in which these six old men asked you thousands of questions. Some of these questions were really tricky and then others were very personal like, "Describe to us your personality." I'm sure, what a thing to ask! Anyways, then after this 15 min. conference they sent us to the cafeteria and we got to eat anything we wanted on the house. That was really nice, but they had already run out of pork chops, so we had chicken instead. Next, we just sat around and waited for their decision which they were supposed to tell us at 8 o'clock. It wasn't until 9 o'clock before they let us know, so we all sat around and watched "Fame" on the big TV screen. So then, when they finally announced the winners, we had to go up stairs to the real Elks meeting and be presented to all of these old men. This is where the embarrassing part comes in. We had to walk through the middle of the floor up to the podium, and the whole time this guy was playing the organ. Then when they announced us he went, "ta-ta-ta-ta" and they took pictures, plus all of this formal stuff. At the end, they wanted the winners to give a short speech (I was about to die), but it turned out that only the first place winners had to; what a relief!

February 22nd, 1982

Oh yes, this is really great! You're not here today and if I would have known I wouldn't have shown up either. I feel really tired and "headachy" today, basically because I haven't gotten much sleep. The reason as to why I didn't get much sleep? Well, I really don't know. The cause is unknown to me except for the fact that it has something to do with my cancer. The thing is that I was helping you all day Saturday and according to my Grandmother, I was sitting in a crumped up position too long. This caused my lungs, which already have problems getting enough oxygen, to start to cramp up. Oh, yes, the problem was that when I got home I started having these stinging things so that I couldn't breathe. It wasn't much fun. But the real problem is that I don't really know what causes this, but nevertheless, I told myself that I'm going to have to kind-of slow down on things and take it easy. That most likely has been my problem.

Greg's father kept a very detailed, daily log on Greg's medical condition, including the last two months of his life. So as not to dwell on the pain and suffering, only a few short glimpses will be shared.

❖

After Greg's last recording in his journal it was discovered that he had fluid in his lungs. This was the beginning of the end. Several more times the lungs filled and had to be drained. His breathing became labored and the pain more intense. Weakness was ever present. He tried to remain positive, but depression hovered; he fought back. Emergency visits to the hospital, as well as overnight stays offered him little hope, only more tests, x-rays and a plea of "just take me home, please." His doctor, however, scheduled another round of radiation and more chemotherapy, but treatments were promptly canceled, due to Greg's ever weakening condition. As a last resort, another trip to Mexico was squeezed in, only for Greg to give up the fight four days after his return.

There was, at this time, no going back and seeing where something could have been done differently. It was finished and God's will was accomplished. Because of the treatment he received in Mexico, Greg needed no pain medication the last days of his life; he fell into a peaceful sleep. This was a blessing for Greg and his family as they waited together for him to pass over from the only home he knew to a home he knew awaited him.

April 15ᵗʰ 1982

A letter written by Greg's Mom to a dear friend abroad.
Greg passed away 6 days later.

I just had to write a quick note from here in southern California. We are just across the border from Mexico where we took Greg back to the clinic. Greg is not doing very well now; he's been in bed about seven weeks and is quite weak. He is breathing with difficulty and is very thin. His right chest is pushed out, possibly due to the tumors and fluids in his chest. He tries so hard to be brave and not give up, but it is difficult when he has so many problems.

Each day we pray that God will give all of us the strength and wisdom for just that one day. We also pray for the doctors, nurses, technicians etc. who deal with Greg, that they will all make the right decisions for our Greg's health. We must depend on God to guide them, as we certainly do not know what to do. We depend on God's guidance in all decisions, small or large.

I truly feel God has guided us until this point and will continue to do so in the future if we will but remain faithful and trust in Him.

We think of you often and love you. Our prayers are with you too. With much love always,

*

We were never alone, ever, in this chapter of Greg's life. There were hundreds of loved ones and friends the world over who walked with us through each page, praying, calling, writing and visiting. Rereading cards, letters, notes and recorded phone calls revives once again the overwhelming and humbling feelings we experienced because of the many expressions of love and concern. There are no words that could even begin to describe this network of support that surrounded us then and continues to do so. Every reminder of these acts of love causes us, once again, to express our most sincere thanks to each and every one of you.

IV

FINAL THOUGHTS

10

CANCER

SOUTH AMERICAN CANCER CURE: In the 60's it was believed that a tea made from the bark of a tabebuia avellanedae tree could possibly cure cancer. Many other books and publications crowded the market with cancer cures such as artificially induced fevers, strict cleansing diets, fasting, vitamin therapy, laetrile, herbs, interferon, metabolic treatments, immune therapy and many more.

The world of modern medicine offered cobalt, chemotherapy, radiation, surgery, transplants, antibodies, combinations of these treatments and other varieties. Because a tumor might have several different kinds of cancer cells within it, the right approach is often difficult, if not impossible, to determine. New methods of treatment are in experiment almost daily.

Cancer was no respecter of nationality or age. Cancer was on a rampage in all countries attacking all ages, and because no one cure seemed to be consistently working, everyone with the disease was searching for a miracle. Greece and other European countries, South America, Mexico and many states in our vast USA offered treatment programs. Who had the answer? How could one find it?

Test the untested. Many treatments were labeled "experimental research" and often a federal grant was available if one was willing to lend his/her body to the newly founded treatment.

Now, make your choice. It was in this era that Greg became ill. Scores of people, friends, family members and doctors suggested ways to deal with Greg's cancer. To do nothing would have been unthinkable; to refuse the wisdom of experienced doctors seemed to express shortsightedness; to delve into the hundreds of "miracle cures" for cancer would have been like trying to ascend the Alps without even an ice pick in hand. To rely on the feelings of the heart seemed irresponsible; the heart wanted to protect from any form of pain or fear. It was like being in the middle of a room surrounded by a panoramic screen flashing enticing procedures for a cancer-riddled body. "Try this one, no this one is better; look over here, no, here, no, here, here." It was overwhelming; it was devastating; it was reality. A decision had to be made, but the path was far too treacherous and narrow. It was like having a rock wall on one side, a bottomless drop on the other and the unknown straight ahead. Darkness already was creeping in from behind; there was no way to go but straight ahead, but how?

For the one who knows not God, this would be the point of ruination and doom. The child of God, on the other hand, waits on the Lord, knowing He is the only One who can sort through the maze when human minds are too clouded to think. Prayers were offered throughout many parts of the world and the Lord led the way, step by step, by step, by step. Everyone knew God could allow healing at any step, with or without treatment, if He so willed. His will would be done; stay on the path with Him.

Greg's treatment began after a biopsy that showed he had osteosarcoma on his knee with lesions already in one lung. Massive doses of chemotherapy along with radiation were injected, dripped and radiated into his already weakened body.

Each treatment with an overnight stay at the university hospital cost approximately $11,000. These treatments were given every two or three weeks, depending on Greg's tolerance. Insurance covered 80% of the costs. Needless to say the group insurance went "belly up" in time and were it not for generous and gracious outpourings of love from brethren and friends around the world it could have led to a financial disaster. All those who found it in their heart to help were and always will be very much appreciated. In time, and without request, Greg was accepted into the clinic research program of the hospital. A grant was offered for this experimental program, covering some of the costs. Just knowing he was being "experimented" on was difficult enough, but knowing these research methods might not work, was a thought unbearable to ponder. Greg accepted each step in his treatment without complaint; he was positive and hopeful.

Because metastasis was found in Greg's lungs at the time of the diagnosis, his chances to survive were diminished. However, one doctor gave Greg a lot of "false" hope, only to have it shatter within a few months. A report from the National Cancer Institute gave cancer patient survival statistics, but where did they get this information? Greg's type of cancer was not listed. It was later revealed in an article on osteosarcoma with metastasis, that these patients had really no chance of survival. Why then did some say Greg could get well? Why did they not spare him all the pain and suffering of the treatments? Why? Maybe there is no human answer. Cancer remains a mystery only God understands. He is and was in control. He knows the needs of each of His children because He created them. He is the good Shepherd. He wins all battles even when they are with the dreaded disease we all call cancer.

Seemingly, much criticism is on the horizon for clinics in other countries with some possible substantiation, but not until one is in a medical labyrinth, where hopes and answers are lost in a spin, does one understand the strong need to pursue other channels. It can be said, by some, to families in such tragic circumstances, that those clinics pick the pockets of their patients. However, it is never mentioned that there might be a clinic with enough concern for the family that after the death of one of their patients they consider a substantial bill paid in full because their services are no longer needed. Greg's younger brother became so frustrated by the attitude and pride of some that he wrote a six page article on "unjust treatment of cancer patients." Where are the answers? The rest is left up to each one's own interpretation.

11

DEATH

There are many wonderful events one looks forward to in life, like the first day of school, a new pair of tennis shoes, that first date, graduation, a new job, marriage, the birth of a child, vacations, holidays and just having the whole family together around the dinner table. These are times to be held dear, forever to be engraved in memory, each one helping to create a piece of foundation for the future.

There is one event however, most do not look forward to or dream about; this is the mere thought of death, a thought too chilling to be allowed to visit the mind for longer than a fleeting moment. Death means separation. It is a severing of a long, loving relationship, a shattering of an enduring friendship, or a parting from a well-respected acquaintance. A place in life suddenly becomes vacant, deserted, still, unable to ever be filled again in the same way. Foreign feelings creep into the heart and invade the mind; sensations of hollowness or abandonment pitch a tent over the soul. Death.

Some look at death as a final good-bye, like locking a door and throwing the key away. From all outward appearances there seems to be a race, a race through all stages of grief in a matter of days, an urgency to forget and go on. But somewhere, somehow, concealed feelings break through and force the heart to reconsider. Death.

Others look upon death with mixed emotions, both fear and relief. Some fear death because of the unknown. Others fear because

of pain, loss of control, not having all things in order or leaving burdens on others. Thoughts of dying before the children are grown or
having to bid farewell to loved ones and familiar surroundings bring
fear. Often the subject of death is not a popular topic, but a dreaded one. It tends to be avoided until it knocks at the door. Death.

Being prepared to enter the open door of death is a blessing
God bestows only on His own. Knowing for certain that God is
watching at the door to receive the faithful, takes away fear and
death's sting loses its threatening force. God waits; He will remain.
Relief is near. Relief is an easing of pain or lightening of a burden,
which death in the Lord truly is. It is a letting go and at the same
time an adhering to, a giving up and a taking on. It is leaving the world
behind and arriving in God's presence. It is a going home. Death.

Another form of relief begins its training before death comes
into view. It is the relief in knowing what lies ahead. This relief is
based on faith, faith in God's power to overcome whatever may
enter the scene. When faith coupled with understanding occupies
more heart spaces than fear, then the soul will know relief even as
a pilgrim on earth, and at the same time yearn to be with God. So,
when death's door slowly begins to creak open, one can truly say,
"I have fought the good fight, I have finished the course, I have kept
the faith; in the future there is laid up for me the crown of righteousness, which the Lord, the righteous Judge, will award to me on
that day." Death. Fear. Relief.

12

IN MEMORY OF

At the moment of death a feeling of urgency sets in. There are so many decisions to be made for a funeral, memorial or graveside service, that time suddenly escapes like vapor. Decisions one had previously hoped would not have to be made, become imminent and seem to multiply quickly. Because few think to educate themselves for such an occasion, it is like being lost in the woods without a compass. It is a very vulnerable time when thinking may be clouded and the feeling of wanting to "just get through it" prevails. It is wise to find a quiet place and take time out for the mind to clear. Hasty considerations, like turning every detail over to funeral professionals, may not be in the best interest of all concerned — it is a contemplative time.

In times of sorrow, when thoughts are scattered, one needs a dear friend or family member to write down the wishes of all involved in the service. This may take several hours, but once recorded, these desires can then be read back to those making the arrangements. This allows everyone to get an overview and at the same time have an active part in the planning and in the sharing of the burdens. Someone close to those in distress may already have had experience in arranging a funeral or memorial service and be able to offer valuable resources. As soon as important decisions have been reached, the funeral home may then get involved. They will be able to aid in fulfilling requests and even offer some suggestions, if desired. Having several present in these final hours of preparation distributes responsibilities among family members as well as those close to the family, lending strength and support when most needed—it is a decisive time.

Just as grieving is personalized, so is a funeral. It is designed to honor the deceased, as well as for family and friends. It is an assembly of those who have come to share memories of the one who has gone on before. It is a time to find comfort and to give comfort. It is a time to fulfill each other's needs, large and small. It is a time of sadness, but also of peace and joy. For God's children, funerals are a place to be surrounded by their support group, matched by no other; it is His design. God is the Master of support and comfort. He has taught His children how to serve one another, not only in times of joy and happiness, but also in the hour of sorrow and death. Hand in hand they will walk through the valley, fearing no evil, for they have each other and they have God; this team lacks nothing—it is a compassionate time.

Funerals do bring about a certain closure. For some it is like the closing of a book after reading the last chapter; it is all over. But for most who mourn, it may be more of a beginning, a beginning of a life alone, or one with a deep vacancy. True supporters will be quick to sense when they are needed; their services may extend over a very long period of time. Abandoning a griever in a critical phase of the grieving process may set them back, whereas remaining by their side will allow them to work through the tangles of grief with assurance, knowing that two or three adjoining hearts are stronger than one alone—it is a supportive time.

When a child is called home to God, leaving siblings in a state of uncertainty, parents have a special opportunity and obligation to be there for each one of them. Possibly, the children were not even told about the seriousness of their sibling's health. Or maybe, death came suddenly when no one was prepared and the entire family was thrown into shock together. Often, parents must first deal with the tragedy themselves before they can even think about helping their children. Again, this is where reaching into the loving resources of those waiting to help can supply security and aid for everyone at the same time. Unique resources close at hand include those offered through the child's siblings. With little guidance, older children can become a source of strength to all. They are quite capable of accepting full responsibility for tasks such as making or answering phone calls, writing letters or thank you notes, rallying around the younger siblings, shopping, cooking or running errands. Keeping busy by helping others is a wonderful self-help method in breaking through the barriers of grief. Neighbors too, who watched the children grow up, are close at hand and feel useful when they can assist in any way. Their homes are not foreign nor are their faces or hearts, their services cannot be underestimated, they are so very valuable. Other family members, if close by, have knowledge of the children's personalities and will be able to spread their arms around the family with warmth and comfort. Christians are also an intricate part of God's family, a family which answers the call of service, day or night, willingly and with love. When one hand reaches out it is met by one or more reaching back. It is a grasp that provides strength and doesn't let go. It holds on as long as it is needed— it is a strengthening time.

Because most young children are accustomed to waiting for their needs to be fulfilled, they may not even know what to ask for when there has been a death in the family, but those with a watchful eye will be able to see and feel their state of distress. Children, too, become very observant, observant of their parents, other siblings and those who come and go around them. They watch and listen, learning treasured lessons while at the same time seeking something that will help relieve their immediate pain and doubt. Each child will try to cope with the loss of a brother or sister in a personal way, but very often needs help. Many times children don't understand why their own flesh and blood had to be taken away from them. Some will openly cry and make their inner feelings known to everyone around them. Others shut themselves out, find a quiet corner or disappear into their room and close the door.

These are all cries for assistance, whether loud or silent, but because parents are generally the focus when a child dies, these pleas can easily be overlooked. Offering a warm and safe atmosphere for children will encourage conversations. Some children will want to write their deepest thoughts on paper, not just one time, but continuously. Writing releases emotions that can be read over and over again, thus aiding in the grief process. Tender sentiments of small children may best be expressed by inviting them to take up crayons, pencils or markers and draw. They are natural artists and will willingly express their feelings on paper. Such expressions may be the first step in their understanding of why they are so sad. Understanding precedes accepting the loss and acceptance is one necessary healer for a grief-stricken soul — it is an understanding time.

When parents themselves are able to take an active part in their children's grief, the family pulls together in a way no one ever thought it would or could. Often, it is a child who will make a very comforting statement to Mom and Dad or to their brothers or sisters. Their hearts have been entwined for many years with that of their deceased sibling; they have much to offer and it should be heard. Therefore, depending on their age, they need to be included in conversations dealing with the death of the one they miss and mourn — it is a reminiscing time.

To ease their fears, children of all ages can also be included in planning the funeral or memorial service. The selections of flowers, songs, poems or readings are areas where children will be able to express their wishes. They may also be allowed to actually arrange the flowers as they arrive for the service. Since most funerals have no set rules, there is plenty of room for designing the service in a personal way, the same way a family would also plan any other important occasion. Each involvement allows the child to do some final act of love for their brother or sister. These acts of kindness grant solace in grief and allow the child, or children, to experience a sense of closure. The funeral then becomes a very important step for children along the path of healing and accepting. The days, months or possibly years that follow will be easier because of the opportunities afforded them through the elementary principles of coping with death. Learning and then doing are marvelous self-confidence builders. Strength and a sense of security will surface each time the children recall to memory their part in helping with the final good-byes to their brother or sister. This contentment will not only soothe their aching hearts, but also help fill in some of the empty spaces — it is an involvement time.

Gregory Dean Earnhart: 1963–1982

In some countries there are strict laws that govern funerals. In others, traditions or customs become the standard by which arrangements are planned. Then there are places that have neither, so the family may proceed according to their own wishes. In the state where Greg passed away, his family was told that embalming was a state law. This, however, was quickly found to be untrue and Greg's body was not embalmed, but kept cool until the day of the funeral. All other arrangements were taken care of by Greg's family and friends, just as Greg would have wanted them to be. Because Greg was a very personal, family oriented young man, he would have chosen those whom he had cried and prayed with, those who never stood over him, but sat alongside; those he could reach out to and those he knew, without a doubt, would surround him in his final hour; they would be the ones to prepare him for burial. These were also some of the ones who helped guide his steps to the bank of the river so he could cross over; now they wanted to plan his last honors. It was to be their final gift to the one they didn't want to let go, but God knew he needed to go — it was time.

Somewhere to the north of Greg's home was a gentleman who hand-carved caskets out of a single piece of wood. These caskets were carefully sculptured out of love for the simple, beautiful, natural woods. Greg's father and uncle drove to the man's workshop and selected one of his pieces of art. It could not have been more fitting for Greg who himself appreciated an artists' finished work — it was perfect. The casket was brought in the family van to Greg's home; there it was placed in the garage to be prepared by those whom Greg would have chosen — his family. His favorite blanket, his own pillow and some things Greg wouldn't have wanted to part with, were carefully placed inside. There were no padded, satin linings and no brass or gold handles. It was a wooden box, plain and simple, but masterfully designed — it was Greg's. The casket was then taken to the funeral home along with Greg's personal clothes. This whole process was not something Greg's family ever thought they would be allowed to do, but it was most certainly the most rewarding — it was fulfilling.

Other preparations for the funeral were be finalized quickly because many, many family members, loved ones and friends made themselves available all hours of the day and night. Greg's aunt and uncle took the younger brothers and sister shopping for clothes and aided in other important, practical ways. Friends of Greg lovingly accepted responsibilities; they were true and kind. The family selected hymns and a dear friend made hundreds of copies to be handed out at the funeral. Greg's older brother designed the program for the service, using a part of the last poster Greg had designed for the fall play. Greg's older sister and husband made many trips to the airport to receive friends and family members coming from afar; they were a pillar of strength in every way. Neighbors, friends and loved ones flowed in and out of the house showering the family with food, flowers and gifts of all kinds. The family's daily needs were not only met before and after the funeral, but also in the following weeks. Everyone fell into his or her designed role like a faithful servant, not expecting to be rewarded, just serving. Surely some of these humble tasks were never acknowledged though they were a necessary part of the whole benevolent effort for the family— it was humbling.

Such overwhelming outpourings of love and compassion wrapped the family like a warm, fuzzy blanket; the ever faithful support group. Decisions were not made alone, for someone was always at hand. Tears could flow naturally because understanding hearts were ever present. It was a time for the family to receive; they would have their opportunity to give. God's love and reassurance were needed. He was gracious. He was evident. He remained— it was comforting.

On Saturday April 24th a memorial service was planned, after which it would be time to carry Greg's body to its final resting place. The skies spread their shades of blue over the white puffy clouds like a magnificent tent. The clouds floated around, allowing the sun to shine down on all those who gathered to express their love for Greg and the family— it was pleasant.

Because of the personal touch in all areas of Greg's illness, death and now his burial, it was only fitting that the family's big green van should serve as a hearse, Greg's older brother as the driver, with his brother-in-law assisting. They drove to the funeral home and loaded the casket in which Greg's body had been placed. The casket was never to be opened again. Greg would have wished it to be so, and so it was— it was good.

The auditorium at the high school, where Greg spent just short of four years, was chosen for the service. Because entertaining was one of his favorite pastimes, the casket was placed on the stage, the old, familiar stage, the stage where Greg once stood and walked, sang and performed in front of massive backdrops he helped create. It was perfect— it was like Greg.

As Greg's supporters filled the rows of seats it was like coming to see Greg's last performance, but he would not appear on this day; he had already retired and God had taken him home. Only the memories of Greg's short life remained, but they filled the auditorium with warmth and vibrancy in very much the same way his performances once did. He lives on in the hearts of his devoted supporters. Their names are recorded in the guest book. They are often remembered— rightly so.

Praise was given to the One who graciously allowed everyone to know Greg and to be a part of their lives. There were no instruments except for those in each heart as they blended together in beautiful songs of heaven, God's goodness, His understanding and watchful care. Greg's uncles and family friends directed the ceremony. The high school's selected chorus also sang a selection of songs they had often sung together with Greg. It was difficult for his friends, as it was for all, but it was just as Greg would have wanted it to be— it was his way.

Greg's older brother and brother-in-law rewrote some words of a well-known song for the service. Greg's brother sang the song in memory of his brother and friend— it was his final farewell.

> Good-bye to you my trusted friend
>> We've known each other since we were nine or ten
>> Together we've climbed hills and trees
>> Learned of love and ABCs
>> Skinned our hearts and skinned our knees
>
> Good-bye my friends it's hard to die
>> When all the birds are singing in the sky
>> Now that the spring is in the air
>> Happy faces every where
>> Think of me and I'll be there

We had joy we had fun
We had seasons in the sun
But the hills that we climbed
Are now seasons of the past time.

Good-bye Mama, please pray with me
I was the clown of our family
You tried to teach me right from wrong
Too much play and too much song
Wonder how I got along

Good-bye Papa, it's hard to die
When all the birds are singing in the sky
Now that the spring is in the air
Pretty children every where
When you touch them I'll be there.

We had joy we had fun
We had seasons in the sun
But the memories and songs
Will to all of you belong
We had joy we had fun
We had seasons in the sun
And the times that we shared
Let me know that you all cared.

Good-bye my friends and loved ones
You gave me love and helped me find the sun
Every time that I was down
You would always come around
And got my feet back on the ground.

Good-bye my friends, it's hard to die
But we will meet again as time goes by
God will call us to come home
To share eternity with Him
I pray that we will all be there.

We had joy we had fun
We had seasons in the sun
And the times that we shared
Proved to me that you all cared.

The family's big green van led the motorcade carrying Greg's body to its final resting place. The chosen cemetery was to the south of Greg's home in a city where his mother grew up and where loving relatives lived. A burial plot was selected on a grassy slope just a few feet above where Greg's grandmother was buried. On the lower edge, towering trees lined a small road that met another and wandered off together. A year later the best friend of Greg's mother was buried just across from Greg. Though massive numbers of graves cover countless rolling hills, there is only one, small place where names are familiar, close to each other, where memories never fade—it was meant to be.

A few closing words were spoken near the flower draped casket after which faithful supporters, one by one, came to express their words of comfort and encouragement. Slowly the numbers dwindled leaving close friends, family and loved ones a few quiet moments to reminisce. This allowed time to talk about being prepared for the day Greg had just met; it will come to all. Greg's little brother lingered by the casket. He did not fully understand what was going to happen to his kind friend and brother, nor did he want to say good-bye. The time had come—it hurt.

Back at the family dwelling guests filled the rooms as well as the back yard with warmth, comfort and laughter. Food brought by neighbors and friends was spread on tables and served with love. It was the final paragraph to the story of a memorable service for Greg. Everything had been done as if Greg were there directing the program. It was his way. It was personal, it was beautiful, it was perfect and it was finished.

Now it was time, once again, to thank God for His mercy, His love, His grace. It was a time to thank Him for allowing Greg to be a part of all those who walked with him, creating memories to live on in dedicated hearts. It was also a time to be grateful for daily reminders of the path, the only path that leads home to God. Though this passageway meanders through the valley of the shadow of death where danger lurks at every bend, those who keep stride with God fear no evil. Like a loving Shepherd He guides His flock into the fold, into His glory, forever. He is the King of glory; thanks be unto Him.

Auf Wiedersehen Greg

Dedicated With Love

In memory of and out of love for Greg some of his loyal friends built a memorial in his honor. Each letter of their message was carefully carved with hands that once offered unselfish aid to a friend who needed them and one they wanted to remember in a very special way. The memorial was placed by the music and art wing of the high school, the wing in which Greg was able to develop and to share some of his talents. A Douglas fir was planted beside it; it was a perfect setting. As the school expanded and the memorial had to make way for the development, a request was made by the school to transfer the words of the memorial onto a plaque and hang it in the foyer of the new Performing Arts Center. The glorious, old auditorium with all the reminders of Greg on stage no longer exists, but the memories of Greg are now in the halls of a new auditorium where Greg's nieces and nephews carry on for him — on stage.

Words of the Memorial

THE DOUGLAS FIR, SYMBOL OF MAJESTY,
EMBODIMENT OF QUIET STRENGTH,
GROWS STRAIGHT AND TRUE. IT GAINS ITS STATURE
THROUGH THE STRUGGLE
TO OVERCOME THE OBSTACLES
TO ITS EXISTENCE AND PROGRESS.
SO ALSO ARE THE NOBEL YOUTH
WILLING TO STAND FOR TRUTH
AS PILLARS OF SILENT STRENGTH
THEY STRUGGLE FOR PROGRESS, FOR IMPROVEMENTS
AND ENLIGHTENMENT
DEDICATED TO: GREGORY EARNHART
WITH LOVE

Memorial to Gregory Earnhart